moroccan modern

I would like to dedicate this book to my mother who, although she is no longer with us, has had a profound effect on my life and the path on which I have travelled. Without her inspiration, warmth, love and devotion to me, I doubt I would be who I am today. I will love her always and her smile remains etched in my memory forever.

And, to my children Jasmine and Ramahl—you complete my life and I cherish you both. May your paths through life be travelled with ease towards your ultimate goals and happiness.

moroccan modern

Hassan M'Souli

photography by
Joe Filshie

NH
NEW
HOLLAND

contents

acknowledgements

The idea of putting together a Moroccan recipe book had been playing on my mind for some time; it was a discussion I had regularly over past years as a chef and restaurateur. My customers were constantly asking me, 'Can I have the recipe for that?' or 'What's in this dish?' After being approached by New Holland through Robynne Millward, my dream was finally to become a reality. I began compiling and correcting already existing recipes and developing new creations.

During this journey I was lucky to have the help and inspiration of those people close to me. The process was very time consuming and took me away from my business. My staff all had to take on extra responsibility to keep Out of Africa running smoothly during my absence, and I thank them all for their efforts and loyalty.

Fuad Mahbood, my head chef, assisted during the preparation and testing of all the recipes in this book and, without his help, the task would have been a little daunting. Fuad's dedication to replicating the Out of Africa taste and quality on a day-to-day basis helps to keep our regulars coming back time and again. Yun and Adil Majdi also went beyond the call of duty in the quest of completing *Moroccan Modern*. With Yun helping Fuad and I in the kitchen, Adil kept everyone happy by managing the floor, in his usual charming manner, and making sure everything ran without a hitch.

The traditional recipes found in this book have been born from my mother's influence, adapted to suit changing tastes and ingredients. The memory of my mother will always remain strong.

I spent hours sitting with my partner Catherine McConachy going through ideas, researching and writing. Catherine typed up my thoughts, was a constant sounding board, offering encouragement and advise. She helped keep my sanity during the whole process, and brought the final manuscript to life.

My beautiful children Jasmine and Ramahl have been very supportive, sacrificing our precious time together to allow me to complete this book. It has been hard for me not to be with my children, but they never complained, always ready to hear about the progress of the book and to share this exciting time with me.

Omar Majdi, through his business Ambiance Interiors, has supplied Moroccan plates, tea pots, glasses and other artifacts which you will see throughout the book. Being my business partner for over 10 years, Omar has been an inspiration, lending support and advice throughout our partnership and friendship.

I would also like to thank my family, both here and in Morocco, for their constant love and encouragement, helping me throughout my career to achieve my life's ambitions. Special mention goes to Susanne, Jessie, Myles, Semo and Joanne, Merieme and Ali. Thank you all for your support.

Thank you to Rita Winiger who supplied ceramic dishes you will see in the some of the photographs, and to Robynne Millward for her dedication in getting *Moroccan Modern* off to a great start, for help with all the food styling and her invaluable advice and support. If I have missed anyone, you all know who you are, and I'd like to thank everyone and anyone who has helped in any way.

introduction

Bustling bazaars bursting with colour, the aroma of fabulous food, swaying palms, exotic palaces and serene mosques, terracotta against Mediterranean blue.

King Hassan II poetically compared Morocco to a desert palm when he said it was 'rooted in Africa, watered by Islam and rustled by the winds of Europe'.

Situated south of Spain, on the north-west coast of Africa, Morocco is one of the three countries which make up the Maghreb ('furthest west') with Algeria and Tunisia. There are two magnificent mountain ranges in Morocco, and the melting snows of the Atlas Mountains feed the rivers which flow down to the lush coastal plains.

Cereals, citrus fruits and vegetables thrive across the vast terrain. Being a coastal country, fish and seafood are also plentiful, while the inland environment is perfect for raising sheep, goats and poultry. With such bountiful natural resources, it is no surprise that of its nearly 25 million people, a vast number of Moroccans are heavily involved in agriculture.

Many think that due to the French and Spanish possession of Morocco in the 19th and 20th centuries, the cuisine of Morocco is heavily influenced by these cultures. Although some of the ideas have been shared, Morocco's culinary origins can be traced directly back to the indigenous Berbers, and to the Arabs who invaded the country in the 7th century AD.

The Arabs introduced many spices such as cumin, paprika and turmeric. Today, many other spices are also used in Moroccan cooking, including saffron, coriander, cardamom and ginger. In traditional recipes, you'll also find ingredients such as walnuts, almonds, preserved lemon, oranges, honey, wheat, olives, figs, prunes and other dried fruits. Moroccans have mastered the art of marrying fruit and meat together, with the subtle use of spices used to enhance a dish rather than mask any of the flavours. This makes it an altogether exotic and rewarding style of cooking.

Moroccan cuisine is based on traditional recipes and techniques, but relies on the cook's intuition. This art is handed down from mother to daughter (or son, as in my case), including secrets such as how to prepare the best couscous.

In this book I share with you all the secrets passed on to me from my mother, along with my wealth of knowledge gained over the years of operating my own restaurants.

The recipes in this book are easy to follow. While some may take a little more time in preparation, the end result is truly worth the effort. Inside, you'll find many traditional favourites, along with some original creations and adaptations. And now, you're invited to make these dishes your own.

The Art of Entertaining —Moroccan Hospitality

*'You will open the door to any stranger and you will bestow your hospitality
on him for three whole days before enquiring of the object of his visit.'*

The art of hospitality is legendary in Morocco, and eating is very much a social ritual, as well as a necessity. When you enter a home, whether it is a wealthy household or a humble Berber tent, you will be greeted with a warm welcome and offered a variety of food. It would be an insult to refuse, and why would you? The hospitality of Morocco is an experience not to be missed, food is always plentiful and wonderfully aromatic and flavoursome.

A handwashing ceremony is performed before the serving of food. The washing of hands is done over a copper basin, and the palms then sprinkled with orange blossom water.

When everyone is seated and the food is ready, the host will pronounce 'Bismillah' (in the name of Allah), which will be repeated by all present at the table. Bread is broken by the host and offered to the guest to use as a 'fork' to scoop up tasty morsels of food from a communal dish.

Moroccans eat using the thumb and first two fingers of their right hand (the left hand is considered unclean), using bread as a utensil. To eat with one finger is said to have the devil's influence, eating with three fingers is a sign of the Prophet, and only gluttons eat with four or five. It is permissible to eat softer food such as couscous with five fingers, or even a spoon.

The midday meal is the main meal (except during the holy month of Ramadan), and abundant servings are the norm. The meal usually begins with a series of hot and cold salads which are followed by a tajine. The heartiest dish, often of lamb or chicken, is next, followed by a large serving of couscous topped with meats and vegetables. Extra servings are always prepared, whether or not visitors are expected. The object of Moroccan hospitality is that everyone will always have more than enough to eat. Leftovers are never wasted and you'll usually find them included with the next meal.

To finish a meal and to cleanse the palate, mint tea is offered, a traditional ceremony in itself.

Generosity is a notable feature of the Moroccan culture. It extends from the table to many other facets of life, including the giving of gifts. Anything in a Moroccan home which is admired by a visitor may be then pressed upon them by the host, and refusal is considered very rude.

If you are invited for a meal it is customary to take a gift and to refuse an invitation is also considered rude.

Moroccans are quick to tell you that the best meals are found in the homes and not at restaurants, and the emphasis in Morocco is clearly on home style hospitality.

the moroccan kitchen

It's amazing when you enter the kitchen of a Moroccan household to find that the most exquisite meals are prepared within the most sparsely equipped kitchens. The Berber cook needs only a canoon (small charcoal brazier), a few clay cooking implements and a great deal of imagination to create a wonderful meal using only small quantities of meat and vegetables. The wealthier urban Moroccans will often use a charcoal fire even when the convenience of gas or electric stoves is available to them.

Some Moroccan kitchens possess all the modern conveniences—refrigerators, freezers, gas burners and a sink with running water—yet they often choose not to use them, reverting to the old traditional ways of cooking. One thing you will notice in almost every Moroccan kitchen is the colourful bottled preserves proudly on display.

Tradition is something that hasn't disappeared in Morocco, the usual country kitchen having earthenware or tin-lined copper cooking pots, wooden mixing bowls and earthenware platters. Tajines are used directly over charcoal held in a brazier, there are no chairs and usually no table, maybe a stool and perhaps a carpet acting as a seat for the cook.

Although you will probably be able to use the equipment you already have in your kitchen, there are a few things that you might like to purchase to make the preparation of your Moroccan meals easier. They are:

couscoussier

A large aluminium, stainless steel or brass pot with a tight fitting colander (with small holes) and a lid, used for the preparation of couscous. Well worth the investment if you want to prepare authentic couscous.

tajine

A tajine is a half-glazed earthenware dish with a pointed, conical lid. Tajines are available in a variety of sizes, from single serve to huge vessels large enough to serve 16–20 guests.

Tajines have several uses. Besides cooking delightfully aromatic and flavoursome dishes, they can also be used as a dish to serve fresh fruits or vegetables. Many Moroccans use them to keep bread fresh. Decorative tajines are also available, but are not used to cook in.

A new tajine needs to be matured, or seasoned, before use. This will remove any earthenware flavour and impregnate the dish with aromatic flavours. It also ensures that the tajine is introduced gently to heat to prevent it from cracking when finally introduced to a gas burner, barbecue or oven.

In the bottom part of the tajine, combine 1 peeled and sliced onion, 4 sliced carrots, 2 peeled cloves of garlic and 1 bay leaf with 1L (32fl oz) of water and 4 tablespoons of olive oil. Cover with the conical lid and cook in a preheated oven 150°C (300°F/Gas 2) for 30–40 minutes. Remove from the oven and allow to cool gradually at room temperature, before removing the ingredients and washing the tajine.

The tajine recipes in this book give instructions to use flameproof casserole dishes as an alternative to cooking in a tajine. This is partly because most people don't have a tajine.

The other reason is that Moroccans traditionally cook over charcoal, which gives a very gentle heat and dishes are cooked for a long time. Standard stove tops can't quite replicate that type of heat, though using a heat diffuser underneath would help. If unsure, you can always transfer your cooked food, beautifully arranged, to a warmed tajine to serve at the table.

mortar and pestle
A small dish and a thick, blunt implement, essential for crushing and blending spices and herbs.

ghorbel
A sieve made of thin wire, muslin or silk, used for sifting flour or semolina grain and straining sauces.

chouaya or chebqua
A hinged grill used for cooking fish or meat on a barbecue or over hot coals.

traditional favourites

mint tea

The national drink of Morocco, mint tea is drunk at any hour of the day. It is an infusion of dried green tea, fresh mint and boiling water. Sugar is added and it is traditionally very sweet.

There are many varieties of mint, and any type may be used. The best quality mint in Morocco is 'mentha viridis' which comes from Meknes or the Zerhoun.

Na'na' (mint) tea is best freshly brewed, the ceremony itself is a fine art and a national symbol.

couscous

Moroccans believe couscous brings God's blessing upon those who consume it, and it is considered the national dish of Morocco. It is made from durum-wheat semolina which is native to the region, formed into small grain-like pieces. The way in which couscous is made and prepared varies among the regions of Morocco depending on the family recipe handed down from generation to generation.

Couscous is widely available from large supermarkets and specialty shops. When buying, choose couscous which is imported from Morocco, or which says 'in the style of the Maghreb' (or similar) on the packet. Most packets will give instructions for 'instant' couscous (soaking in boiling water or stock), but for the best, most authentic results follow the instructions given on page 175.

B'stilla

A traditional savoury/sweet pastry, regarded as the crowning dish of Moroccan cuisine. B'Stilla is served to newlyweds the morning after their wedding night to symbolise their family's wish that life together should be as sweet as this dish. It is made in three layers, comprising shredded pigeon (we used chicken), glazed onion and almond, and creamy egg with orange blossom water. These are enclosed in, and separated by, layers of very thin pastry called warka. Filo can be used as a substitute. When cooked, B'stilla is dusted heavily with cinnamon and icing sugar. This dish truly is a labour of love, time consuming but with worthwhile results.

tajine

A tajine is an earthenware dish with a conical lid, widely used in Morocco to cook a stew-like dish which is also called a tajine (the same way a stew cooked in a casserole dish is called a casserole). These superbly aromatic meat, poultry, seafood or vegetable stews prepared in a tajine are a regular part of the Moroccan menu. The design of a tajine allows the food to steam and simmer slowly, giving each dish a distinctive flavour with an amazing aroma when the lid is lifted. You can serve a tajine straight from the stove to the table, adding to the charm of this Moroccan favourite.

Harissa

A fiery hot paste or sauce made with red chillies. It is served to enhance salads, cooked fish, meat and poultry, and is an automatic addition to couscous. There are several different ways to make Harissa, being one of those recipes passed down through the family. I use a combination of fresh red chillies with red capsicum (bell pepper)—the more capsicum (bell pepper) you use, the milder the flavour—along with herbs, to create my own unique version of this Moroccan favourite.

Bread

Bread (*khubz*), the most basic and essential food, is sacred in Morocco. Traditional Moroccan bread is a round, dense rustic loaf made from wholemeal flour. The women of the household make the dough early in the morning. It is given a distinctive mark to indicate which family it belongs to, then taken to a communal oven for baking.

Beghrir

For a delicious Moroccan breakfast, try this yeasty semolina pancake with a distinctive honeycomb appearance. They are usually served with butter and honey, but are also great with dried fruit, or fruit conserves (jellies). You could also serve these pancakes with savoury toppings.

Charmoula

A sauce or marinade with a combination of flavours including chilli, paprika, saffron, ginger, bay leaves, onion, cumin, garlic, parsley, coriander, preserved lemon and olive oil.

Charmoula (sometimes known as chermoula) is made differently depending on the recipe handed down through the family, or exchanged between cooks, but the principles remain the same. The flavours are used to enhance the natural flavour of the food, not to mask it. Almost all versions of charmoula include chopped parsley, coriander and onion plus an assortment of spices. There are three charmoula recipes in this book. Two are marinades and one is a charmoula sauce which can be used with tajines, vegetable dishes or simply stirred through your favourite pasta.

key ingredients

If you are planning to cook Moroccan food, you will find there are certain ingredients used time and time again. Listed here are those ingredients with a brief description and, in some cases, their history. These ingredients are the essence of the flavour of Moroccan cuisine.

Almonds

The almond tree is a native of the warmer parts of western Asia and North Africa, and is now cultivated in all the countries bordering the Mediterranean, with Spain and Italy being particularly large producers. The fruit of the almond tree (which surrounds the nut) is tough and inedible even when ripe. When fully ripe, the fruit dries and splits, and the almond drops out. The shell is a yellowish buff colour, the outer surface usually pitted with small holes, and inside is the almond kernel. There are different sorts of almonds varying in size and shape, but the main distinction for cooking is the difference between sweet and bitter almonds.

Sweet almonds are the type commonly found in supermarkets, and are used for the recipes in this book. They are available whole, sometimes with the thin brown skin still attached, or blanched (with the skin removed). If for some reason you cannot find blanched almonds, you can blanch them yourself by soaking in boiling water for 5 minutes. The skins should slip off easily. Dry thoroughly before using.

If ground almonds are required, you can grind them yourself for the freshest result, though ground almonds are readily available.

Bitter almonds have a completely different taste with no similarity to sweet almonds. Raw bitter almonds are likely to be poisonous and shouldn't be taken in large quantities. Bitter almond in small quantities is sometimes used as flavouring in sweet dishes and biscuits. Almonds are valuable as a food source, providing energy and nutrients. They are high in fat, though the fat in almonds, as with other nuts, is not saturated fat and is considered a 'good' fat.

argan oil

This oil is worth a mention, although at this stage, it is not available in many countries outside Morocco. It has an interesting story and is worth trying, should you get the opportunity to visit Morocco. The argan tree (*argania spinosa*) is not very well known outside Morocco, in fact many Moroccans have never heard of it, as it grows only in the south west, between Essouira and Agadir. But in this area of around 700–800,000 hectares, there are about 21 million argan trees.

The argan tree is thorny and reaches heights of around 8–10 metres. It lives longer than olive trees and requires no cultivation. The trunk of the tree is twisted and gnarled, allowing goats to climb and feed on the leaves and fruit.

The fruit from the argan tree is similar in appearance to an olive, only larger and rounder, containing a nut with a very hard shell which, in turn, contains 1–3 almond-shaped kernels. Argan oil is produced from these kernels.

When goats eat the fruit, the flesh is digested and the nuts get excreted. The nuts are then collected, each nut cracked open and the kernels removed and then pressed for oil. The oil is often mixed with honey and ground almonds to make a paste called amalou, which is served as a dip for breakfast in Berber households, with a taste similar to peanut butter.

Argan oil has a reddish tinge, slightly darker than olive oil, with a rich nutty flavour. It is said to have medicinal qualities, helping to lower cholesterol, improve circulation and aid the immune system. It is used in cooking and there is increased interest in its possible use in cosmetics. The production of argan oil is managed largely by women and is very much a cottage industry, the oil commands a high price, due to the time-consuming production.

chickpeas (garbanzos)

One of Nature's truly perfect foods, chickpeas (garbanzos) are a great source of protein and contain very little fat. They contain complex carbohydrates, fibre (including the soluble fibre that may lower cholesterol), B vitamins and minerals. Chickpeas (garbanzos) originated in the Middle East, and they are used widely in Moroccan cuisine. They have a delicate nut-like flavour making them a wonderful addition to salads, couscous dishes, meat dishes and with vegetable soups and stews. They can also be roasted for snacks, or processed to make dips. Chickpeas (garbanzos) can be purchased dried (in which case they need to be soaked, preferably overnight, before cooking), or ready for use in a can, although Moroccans would not normally use canned chickpeas.

chillies

The world's most cultivated spice crop and part of our worldwide culture. Maguelonne Toussaint-Samat wrote: 'the last spice to be revealed to the world at large, chilli has in a way become the superlative among spices'.

The history of chillies dates back to around 9000 years ago. They were first cultivated and used in cooking in Mexico and Central America. Christopher Colombus discovered this unusual food in America back in 1492, introducing them to Spain in 1493. The Spanish and Portuguese traders introduced chilli to Africa, Arabia and Asia, and in less than two centuries chillies were in use worldwide.

Chillies come from the Solanaceae (or nightshade) family. Part of this huge family is the Capsicum genus—and that's where the chillies fit in. At least 200 varieties of chilli have now been identified and all are an excellent source of vitamins A and C. The active ingredients that make chillies 'hot' are called 'capsaicinoids', and capsaicin was the first one to be isolated, back in 1876. Capsaicin is found on the seeds, and in fragile glands on the internal white partitions, or ribs, of the fruit or berry. The capsaicinoids tend to be very soluble in fats and alcohol, and very insoluble in water.

The heat of the chilli has the effect of stimulating the palate and increasing blood circulation. This causes the body to sweat which, in turn, has a cooling effect—this is why chillies are so dominant in tropical regions.

When buying fresh chillies, be sure that the skin is firm and crisp. Dried chillies are used when specific results are required (drying intensifies the flavours of the fresh chilli). Look for dried chillies that are a good, even colour and are not broken.

citrus fruits

Fresh oranges, lemons and limes are all used frequently in Moroccan cooking, adding sweetness or zesty flavours. Everything from the rind, pulp and juices are used.

coriander (cilantro)

Also known as Chinese parsley, coriander (cilantro) has a totally different taste to that of parsley. Native to Southern Europe and the Middle East, coriander is now grown all over the world and is one of the most ancient of herbs, its use in both cooking and medicine dating back thousands of years.

There is a huge distinction between the green leaf and the ripe seed, with the flavour being completely different. The coriander seed is spherical in shape, is easily split in two and varies in colour when ripe from cream to pale green or brown. You can buy coriander seed in most supermarkets, either whole or ground. Keep in mind that coriander seed can go stale and lose its flavour, so buy in small quantities and for the best flavour grind it yourself, as required. The flavour is sweet and aromatic.

Bunches of green coriander (cilantro) are easily recognised in your supermarket, the aroma being quite unique. The bright green leaves are fan-like and delicate. Do not dry coriander (cilantro) leaves, they are best used fresh, but can be quick frozen or preserved with salt in oil. Use the leaves in salads, tajines, couscous dishes and as a garnish. The stalks are great for use in flavouring stocks.

dates

The date palm is one of the oldest fruit trees in the world. It is mentioned in the Qur'an and the Bible. There are around 100 million date palms worldwide, of which 62 million can be found in the Arab world. The place of origin is uncertain, some claim that the date palm first originated in Iraq, while others believe that it originated in Saudi Arabia.

Dates are the fruit of the date palm. They are dark reddish brown in colour and oval in shape, with a wrinkled skin coated with a sticky, waxy film. Dates grow in clusters below the fronds on a date palm tree. A single cluster can hold 600 to 1700 dates. Date palms can grow as tall as 100 feet and reach an average age of about 150 years.

The date palm is a perennial. The females normally begin to bear dates within an average of five years from the time of planting, and stay in production for over 60 years. On a commercial scale, the Middle

East and North Africa are the major date palm producing areas in the world. The fruit of the date palm is delicious and can be used in sweet or savoury dishes. Dates can be found fresh or dried; it is much better to use fresh dates where available.

ginger

One of the best known of all spices. The plant has long leaves and grows to around 3 foot high, with flowers that are mainly yellow with a purple lip and decorative spots. The root of the plant, which is the spice, is known as a 'hand', as it looks like a swollen hand with deformed fingers. When buying fresh ginger root, make sure it is firm and not shrivelled. As powdered forms of ginger may not be the best quality, the dedicated cook will use whole dried ginger to produce their own powder. Ground ginger adds a more mellow flavour than the fresh root, and is commonly used in Moroccan cooking.

honey

The beehive would have to be one of the world's most efficient manufacturing plants, when you consider that bees may visit more than two million flowers to gather enough nectar to make just 500g (1lb) of honey. The colour and flavour of honey differs depending on which blossoms the bees gather their nectar from. There are numerous varieties of honey available, with the lighter coloured honeys usually being milder in flavour. Honey is primarily composed of fruit sugar, glucose and water but also contains other sugars as well as trace enzymes, minerals, vitamins and amino acids. Honey is also said to have medicinal qualities. The annual production of honey in Morocco is estimated at 10,000 tonnes, with most of the honey being consumed locally; only small quantities of orange honey are exported. Moroccans have a very sweet tooth and use honey lavishly. Moroccan honey is thick, with an aromatic, herbal flavour.

olives

The branch of the olive tree is a symbol of peace, and the olive tree has been considered sacred as far back as the 17th century BC. Native to the Mediterranean area, the olive tree thrives in subtropical zones including the Mediterranean, United States, Latin America and, more recently, in Australia and New Zealand.

Fresh olives are quite bitter and inedible, and need to be treated to draw out the bitterness before being consumed. The final flavour of the olives depend on how ripe the fruit is when picked, and how it is processed after picking. As with other varieties of fruit, there are many different types of olives and availability will depend on where you live and shop. The most general difference between olives is the colour. Green olives are picked when young and not yet ripe, and therefore have a firm texture. 'Black' olives (which actually can vary in colour from beige to a dark purple) are picked at different stages of ripeness—generally the darker the more ripe they are. Most tree ripened olives are used for oil, the rest are cured in a brine or salt-cured and then usually packed in olive oil or a vinegar solution. The Greek

Kalamata and the French Niçoise olives are two of the more popular imported ripe olives. Dry-cured olives (as used frequently in Morocco) are packed in salt which removes most of the moisture and creates dry, wrinkled fruit. These olives are great flavoured with Harissa (see page 26). We could go on and on about olives, as their popularity has spread worldwide over the past decade. No longer just used sparingly on top of your pizza, olives are a taste sensation on their own. Try some of the delicious recipes in this book using olives—you'll be delighted by the taste.

olive oil

The word 'oil' comes from olive. The finest quality extra virgin olive oil is cold pressed from the best fruits, and can be yellow or green, with flavours ranging from delicate to peppery, depending on the fruit. Subsequent pressings, usually made under heat, produce lower grade oil. It is important to purchase a good olive oil, so look for labels that say 'first cold pressed'. The quality of olive oil, like wine, can also vary from year to year. Choosing a good quality olive oil also comes down to personal preference, some will prefer light oil with a delicate perfume, others may prefer the heavy, fruity flavours. If you do like olive oil you will probably keep both, using each for different purposes. More flavoursome oils may be desirable for use in dressings, whereas more subtle oils are good to use for cooking. Used widely in Moroccan cooking, olive oil adds flavour to a variety of dishes, both cooked and uncooked.

orange blossom water

The best orange blossom water comes from the Dades Valley in Morocco (on the Eastern side of the Atlas Mountains). The Dades River runs through the heart of the valley, with orange and almond orchards lining its banks. Distillation of orange blossom water is one of the area's main industries. Most countries tend to import orange blossom water and it can be found in specialty stores as well as the gourmet section in some of the larger supermarkets.

parsley

This is such a common herb, so adaptable that it grows in almost any climate. There are several varieties, the two most common being flat leaf parsley (also known as continental parsley) and curly leaf parsley. Some say the flat leaf variety has the better flavour, with the curly leaf being more attractive as a garnish. In this book the flat leaf variety is preferred. Wash and dry thoroughly, and pick the leaves from the stalks.

Moroccans tend to use parsley more as a vegetable than herb, using large quantities in recipes, and also adding it as a garnish.

pomegranate

This exotic fruit probably originated in Persia, and is a common ingredient in Moroccan cooking. The beautiful red seeds are used both as an ingredient and a garnish, for sweet and savoury dishes. To extract the seeds from the fruit, cut in quarters lengthways. Using your fingers, scoop the seeds out into a bowl, leaving behind the white membrane. Break up the fruit as you go, to expose more seeds. One medium pomegranate will yield about 1 cup (150g/5oz) of seeds.

preserved lemons

These are one of the most widely used ingredients of Moroccan cooking. In Morocco they are sold loose in the souks, and you can buy them in jars from specialty shops. In this book, we show you how to preserve your own, and it is worth remembering that they make a great gift idea. Essential in a Moroccan kitchen, they are used in lamb and vegetable tajines, in recipes for chicken, in salads, with couscous and chickpeas, in salad dressings and as a garnish. The texture and unique pickled taste cannot be duplicated with fresh lemon or lime juice. Thin-skinned lemons are the best to use. They are scrubbed and soaked and finally preserved in rock salt (see recipe page 29). Sometimes you will see a sort of lacy, white substance on the preserved lemons in the jar, this is harmless but it should be rinsed off just before the lemons are used, for appearance sake (very important when preparing Moroccan food—feed all the senses!). Preserved lemons are rinsed before use to rid them of their salty taste. Different recipes use different parts of the lemon. Some ask for just the flesh, some just the rind, and others the juice. If the juice is asked for, it means to squeeze it from the preserved lemon, not use the liquid in the jar.

rose water

Although not used as frequently as orange blossom water, rose water is often used in Moroccan cooking. The best rose water in Morocco is also from the Dades Valley. Also found in specialty stores and the gourmet section of some of the larger supermarkets.

warka

Warka is a paper thin, traditional pastry used in dishes such as B'stilla. It is very labour intensive to make and not widely available ready made. We have used filo pastry in these recipes, which is the closest substitute and easy to buy.

Note: Unless otherwise stated, all the herbs used in the recipes in this book are fresh, rather than dried.

spices

Spices are a common staple in most pantries, and are somewhat taken for granted, left to sit on the shelf for months or even years. If you want your Moroccan dishes to be as aromatic and flavoursome as they should be, rethink your spice shelf. Look for a supplier or specialist who knows their wares, or at least shop where there is a high turnover. Ground spices become stale quite quickly, so it is worth buying whole spices and grinding your own. You can do this in a mortar and pestle, or in a spice grinder. Lightly toast whole spices in a dry frying pan to develop the flavour and aroma before grinding.

If you are buying ground spices, only purchase quantities that you think you will use up fairly quickly.

Anise seed (Aniseed)
This is one of the oldest known spices, closely related to cumin and fennel. It is native to the Middle East and eastern Mediterranean and has a bittersweet, strong fruity flavour with a hint of liquorice. It is used whole or ground in breads and sweets, or whole in soups and stews.

cayenne pepper
A fiery hot spice ground from the flesh and seeds of the cayenne chilli. It is popular in the dishes of southern Morocco.

cinnamon
Cinnamon is the soft inner bark of the cinnamon tree. As the bark dries and contracts it is rolled into tight quills and has an aroma reminiscent of a tropical jungle, with a warm, sweet and intense flavour. Sold as cinnamon sticks or quills, they are relatively soft and easy to grind. There are different grades of cinnamon. If you can find a reputable spice supplier or specialist, ask for the best quality cinnamon. Powered or ground cinnamon, available from the supermarket, is convenient but becomes stale quickly. Cinnamon is used in both sweet and savoury dishes in Moroccan cooking.

cumin
A member of the parsley family. Cumin seeds have a distinctive strong aroma and a slightly bittersweet, assertive and lingering warm, earthy flavour. Cumin is among the most flavourful spices used and is commonly used with meats, lamb and chicken.

paprika
A fine reddish powder made by grinding dried, relatively mild types of chilli. Paprika is labelled either sweet or hot. Use the one specified in the recipe.

Ras el Hanout

A complex and distinctive mix of spices and herbs originating in the Meghribi villages of North Africa. Ras el hanout translates as 'head of shop' (roughly meaning the best in the shop) and the recipe varies according to who makes it. Most versions list 20 or so spices but specific quantities are a much-guarded secret from one spice shop to the next, where blending is considered a special art. It is used with meat, game, poultry and couscous. You will find a simple recipe in this book (see page 42) or you can purchase it ready-mixed at some specialty stores.

Saffron

The most expensive spice in the world fortunately goes a long way. Derived from the stamens of the saffron crocus, it can be used either whole (as threads) or in a powdered form, giving a distinctive colour and flavour. Saffron contains essential oils which provide its flavour, as well as a yellow dye which is soluble in water. Most dishes require only very small quantities of saffron.

Sesame Seeds

Sesame seeds come from an herbaceous tropical plant native to Assyria and are one of the world's oldest spices, being known since circa 3000BC. They have a high oil content and a nutty flavour that becomes pronounced after dry roasting or frying. Used in breads, desserts and as a garnish for savoury dishes.

Turmeric

Turmeric is native to Southeast Asia, though today it is grown in tropical climates throughout the world. It has a rhizome which externally appears similar to ginger, though the flesh is the characteristic bright yellow-orange. The rhizomes are boiled, then dried in the sun for about two weeks. The outer skin is scrubbed off and the dried flesh is ground into a powder. It was used as a dye in ancient times—although not very successfully, as it is not colour fast, although it is the cheapest and most common yellow dye available. Turmeric is used mainly to colour food, and is used in curries and curry powders. Do not use turmeric as a substitute for saffron. This is a huge misconception, because even though the yellow colour it imbues is similar, the flavour is not alike. The result of substituting turmeric for saffron in a recipe could be disastrous.

preserves, sauces, dips and dressings

Harissa

Makes about 4 cups

500g (1lb) small hot red chillies, stalks removed
2 large red capsicums (bell peppers),
roasted and peeled
1 Preserved Lemon (see page 29)
3 garlic cloves

½ bunch coriander (cilantro), chopped
2 tablespoons ground cumin
1 tablespoon salt
olive oil, to cover

Mince the chillies, roast capsicums (bell peppers), Preserved Lemon and garlic by hand or in a food processor. Mix with the coriander (cilantro), cumin and salt until well combined. Let the mixture stand for 1 hour, then transfer to a preserving jar and cover with oil. Store indefinitely in the refrigerator.

Yoghurt, mint and sultana Dressing

Makes about 1¼ cups

1 cup (250g/8oz) natural yoghurt
½ cup (20g/⅔oz) mint leaves
½ cup (60g/2oz) sultanas (golden raisins)

1 tablespoon lemon juice
pinch salt
¼ teaspoon white pepper

Process the yoghurt, mint and sultanas in a blender until smooth and creamy. Stir through the lemon juice, salt and pepper.

  Use tossed through green summer salads with citrus fruits and walnuts, or your own combination of salad with fruits and nuts.

Opposite: Harissa

moroccan preserved lemons

Makes 10

10 thin skinned lemons	8 cardamom pods
1½ cups (480g/16½oz) rock salt	2 small red chillies, optional
1L (32fl oz) boiling water	2 bay leaves, optional
juice of 1 lemon	olive oil, to cover

Scrub the lemons well and soak in water for about 3 days, changing the water daily (this disperses the gas and acids contained in the fruit). Remove from the water and cut four pockets end to end into each lemon, being careful not to slice right through.

Holding a lemon over a bowl (to catch any juice and salt), fill the pockets generously with rock salt, and arrange in a 2L (64fl oz) preserving jar. Repeat with remaining lemons.

Cover the lemons with boiling water. Add the leftover salt and juice, lemon juice and cardamom pods. Chillies and bay leaves may also be added for flavour and decoration, if you like.

Leave the jar for a few minutes to ensure that most of the air bubbles are released. Pour over a thin layer of olive oil to cover the surface. Seal tightly, and store for at least 1 month prior to use.

Correctly preserved lemons can be stored for years.

Note: Alternatively, you could put these into 2 x 1L (32fl oz) jars.

charmoula with preserved lemon

Makes about 4 cups

This version of charmoula works particularly well with poultry,
and is wonderful with grilled or baked fish.

1 teaspoon cumin seeds	¾ cup (185ml/6fl oz) extra virgin olive oil
2 red onions, diced	½ teaspoon saffron threads
4 large garlic cloves, crushed	1 teaspoon ground paprika
1 cup coriander (cilantro), finely chopped	1 teaspoon freshly ground black pepper
1 cup flat leaf parsley, finely chopped	1 teaspoon sea salt
2 red birds eye chillies, finely chopped	olive oil, to cover
1 Preserved Lemon, diced (see page 29)	

Mix all the ingredients thoroughly. Spoon into a jar and cover with a film of olive oil.
Keep in the refrigerator for up to 7 days.

avocado dip

Serves 4

½ red or white onion	¼ teaspoon minced red chilli
1 large avocado	½ teaspoon lemon juice
½ garlic clove, crushed	1 tablespoon chopped chives
½ tomato, diced	salt, to taste
½ teaspoon ground black pepper	

Finely dice the onion. Remove the flesh from the avocado and mash with a fork, add all the other ingredients and mix until well combined. Season with salt, to taste.

moroccan dried black olives with harissa

Makes 500g (1 lb)

500g (1lb) Moroccan Dried Black Olives (see page 39)	½ cup Harissa (see page 26)

Soak the olives in cold water overnight to remove excess salt, drain and allow to dry. Combine the olives in a bowl with the Harissa. Store in a sterilised airtight jar in the refrigerator. This is an excellent appetiser with a glass of wine or beer. Great for summer barbecues.

charmoula marinade

Makes about 3 cups

I tablespoon dried crushed chilli

I tablespoon sweet paprika

I teaspoon chopped fresh ginger

½ teaspoon saffron threads

2 onions, diced

2 bay leaves

I tablespoon ground cumin

2 garlic cloves, chopped

2 tablespoons chopped flat leaf parsley

2 tablespoons chopped coriander (cilantro)

½ Preserved Lemon (see page 29), sliced thinly

½ cup (125ml/4fl oz) olive oil

juice of ½ lemon

Mix all the ingredients together thoroughly, and leave for half an hour prior to use. The Charmoula can be stored in the refrigerator for up to 7 days.

spiced mixed nuts

Makes 3 cups

2 tablespoons oil

I cup (150g/5oz) raw cashews

I cup (150g/5oz) blanched almonds

I cup (125g/4oz) pine nuts

I teaspoon salt

½ teaspoon hot paprika

2 teaspoons ground coriander

Heat oil in a wok over a medium gas flame and fry the nuts until golden. Drain on absorbent paper. Combine the remaining ingredients and toss through the nuts until well coated. Serve hot or cold with drinks.

Spiced Mixed Nuts

Charmoula Marinade

Tomato
Charmoula
Sauce

Moroccan Dried Black
Olives with Harissa

Sweet Chickpeas (Garbanzos)

eggplant (aubergine) dip

Serves 6–8

1 large eggplant (aubergine)	juice of 1 lemon
2 tablespoons tahini	3 tablespoons flat leaf parsley, chopped
2 garlic cloves, peeled	½ cup (125ml/4fl oz) olive oil
1 medium onion, chopped	salt and freshly ground black pepper, to taste
¼ cup (40g/1½oz) fresh breadcrumbs	flat leaf parsley, to garnish
¼ cup (60g/2oz) natural yoghurt	flat bread, to serve

Preheat the oven to 190°C (375°F/Gas 5). Pierce the eggplant (aubergine) with a skewer and bake for 45 minutes, until soft. Cut the eggplant (aubergine) in half lengthways and drain off any liquid.

Scoop out flesh and place into a food processor with the tahini. Process for 1 minute.

Add the garlic, onion, breadcrumbs, yoghurt, lemon juice and parsley, process to combine.

With the machine running, gradually add the olive oil. Season with salt and pepper to taste. Transfer to a bowl and garnish with extra parsley if desired. Serve with flat bread.

olive tapenade

Makes about 3 cups

150g (5oz) Kalamata olives, pitted	⅓ cup (15g/½oz) basil leaves
150g (5oz) green olives, pitted	freshly ground black pepper, to taste
3 tablespoons extra virgin olive oil	sliced French baguette, to serve
2 garlic cloves	2 ripe tomatoes, seeded and diced
1 tablespoon capers	basil leaves, to garnish
2 tablespoons lemon juice	

Combine olives, olive oil, garlic, capers, lemon juice and basil leaves in a food processor and process until smooth. Season to taste with black pepper. Serve on slices of French baguette, topped with fresh diced tomatoes. Garnish with extra basil leaves.

mushroom tapenade

Makes about 4 cups

2 cups (500ml/16fl oz) vegetable stock	2 tomatoes, seeded and diced
2 tablespoons olive oil	2 tablespoons tomato paste (tomato concentrate)
1 medium onion, finely chopped	1 cup (250ml/8fl oz) tomato sauce (ketchup)
2 garlic cloves, crushed	½ cup basil leaves, chopped
500g (1lb) button mushrooms, finely chopped	sliced French baguette, to serve

Place the stock into a saucepan and bring to the boil. Reduce the heat slightly and cook until reduced by half.

Heat the oil in a frying pan over medium heat and fry the onion and garlic until soft. Add mushrooms and cook for 1–2 minutes or until softened. Add tomatoes, tomato paste, tomato sauce and reduced stock. Bring to the boil over a high heat, reduce heat and simmer for 10–15 minutes or until the mixture thickens. Stir in the basil leaves. Serve with sliced French baguette.

semi-dried tomato and preserved lemon dressing

Makes 1L (32fl oz)

1 cup (150g/5oz) semi dried tomatoes	½ teaspoon saffron threads
2 Preserved Lemons (see page 29), flesh only	1 tablespoon sugar
1 cup (45g/1½oz) basil leaves	2 cups (500ml/16fl oz) extra virgin olive oil
1 tablespoon freshly ground black pepper	1 cup (250ml/8fl oz) red wine vinegar
1 tablespoon sea salt	

Combine the tomatoes, Preserved Lemon flesh, basil, black pepper, salt, saffron and sugar into a food processor. Process until smooth, then with the motor running gradually add the olive oil and vinegar, alternating a little at a time. Continue to process to make a smooth dressing. Store in the refrigerator for around 3 months.

Bissara Dip

Serves 8–10

1 cup (250ml/8fl oz) extra virgin olive oil
1 onion, grated
2 tablespoons minced garlic
500g (1lb) dried split broad beans (fava beans)
1.5L (48fl oz) water
2 tablespoons ground cumin

1 tablespoon sweet paprika
1 tablespoon white pepper
salt, to taste
1 tablespoon cumin seeds, roasted and crushed
extra virgin olive oil and bread, to serve

Heat half the oil in a large saucepan, and fry the onion, garlic and broad beans until the onion is soft. Add 1L (32fl oz) of the water and simmer for 30 minutes until the beans are tender, adding more water as needed.

Make a paste of the ground cumin, paprika and white pepper with half a cup of water. Add the paste to the broad beans, cook for a further 15 minutes until thickened, stirring regularly (add a little more water if necessary and make sure the mixture doesn't stick to the bottom of the pot). Add salt to taste and stir in the remaining olive oil.

Garnish with roasted cumin seeds and drizzle with a little olive oil. Serve with warm crusty bread or warmed lavash bread.

tomato charmoula sauce

Makes about 8 cups

This simple, tasty sauce is great with most seafood, particularly sardines and mussels.
It makes a delicious base for a pasta marinara sauce.

1 tablespoon olive oil	juice of ½ lemon
2 garlic cloves, chopped	2 tablespoons chopped flat leaf parsley
2 brown onions, diced	2 tablespoons chopped coriander (cilantro)
4 x 400g (14oz) cans crushed tomatoes	salt and freshly ground black pepper, to taste
1 tablespoon ground cumin	

Heat the olive oil in a large saucepan, and fry the garlic and onion until soft. Add the tomatoes, cumin, and lemon juice. Simmer for 20 minutes, stirring occasionally.

Stir through the parsley and coriander (cilantro), remove from the heat. Season with salt and pepper to taste.

This sauce can be stored in the refrigerator for up to 7 days, or frozen.

chickpea (garbanzo) dip

Serves 6–8

400g (14oz) can chickpeas (garbanzos), drained	freshly ground black pepper, to taste
⅓ cup (90g/3oz) tahini	1 tablespoon finely chopped flat leaf parsley, optional
2 garlic cloves, crushed	flat bread, to serve
juice of 2 medium lemons	
1 cup (250ml/8fl oz) extra virgin olive oil	

Combine the chickpeas, tahini and garlic in a food processor and process until smooth. With the machine running, gradually add the lemon juice and olive oil.

Season with pepper to taste. Transfer to a bowl, and serve sprinkled with continental parsley, if desired. Serve with flat bread.

yoghurt dip

Serves 6–8

2 cups (500g/1lb) natural yoghurt
1 small Lebanese cucumber
2 garlic cloves, crushed
2 teaspoons finely chopped dill

1 tablespoon lemon juice
1 teaspoon roasted Anise Seed (aniseed), ground
salt and freshly ground black pepper, to taste

Place the yoghurt into a muslin-lined sieve over a bowl, cover and refrigerate for 1–2 hours. Do not squeeze. Discard liquid from yoghurt.

Cut the cucumber in half lengthways. Scoop out and discard the seeds, coarsely grate the flesh. Place into a medium bowl with the yoghurt, and stir through the remaining ingredients. Serve with flat bread, as a dipping sauce for vegetables, or as a side dish.

moroccan dried black olives

Makes 20kg (40lb)

Fresh olives are washed and placed in baskets with alternating layers of dry salt (equivalent to 15% of the weight of the olives). The result is an olive that is salty but not very bitter, with a wrinkled appearance like a raisin. Eat them as they are, use in numerous dishes or marinate and serve as an appetiser.

20kg (40lb) fresh black olives
4kg (8lb) rock salt
peanut oil, or nut oil of choice

Clean the olives and throw away any that are over-ripe or crushed. Mix with the rock salt and leave to drain in a reed basket, putting several large stones on top of the olives to press. They will exude a black liquid.

After 5 days, spread the olives on a plastic cloth and place in the sun for a whole day. Put them back into the basket, with stones on top for another 5 days. Repeat this process 3 more times. After the third time, put the olives in the sun for 2 days, then mix the olives with just enough oil to coat. They are now ready to eat, or marinate as desired. These olives will keep in the refrigerator for up to 3 months.

creamy white
vegetable sauce

Serves 4

1 cup (250ml/8fl oz) vegetable oil	1 tablespoon ground turmeric
4 garlic cloves, crushed	1 tablespoon ground coriander
4 onions, diced	1 tablespoon finely chopped red chilli
1 cup (90g/3oz) desiccated coconut	1.5L (48fl oz) hot water
1 tablespoon whole fresh lime leaves or lime zest	2 x 400ml (13fl oz) cans coconut cream
2 cinnamon sticks	2 tablespoons rice flour
2 tablespoons black mustard seeds	1 bunch coriander, chopped

Heat the oil, fry the garlic, onions, coconut, lime leaves, cinnamon and mustard until the onion is soft. Add the turmeric, ground coriander, and chilli and fry for a couple of minutes, until fragrant.

   Add the water and coconut cream, and bring to the boil. Reduce the heat and simmer for about 15 minutes. Stir in the rice flour to thicken, then the fresh coriander.

   This sauce is delightful served with fish and/or your choice of steamed vegetables.

smen (aged butter)

Makes 900g

In Morocco there are two types of Smen. One is a preserved clarified butter used mainly for sweet dishes, and the other (Smen Mallah) is salted and then preserved. This is used to season various kinds of couscous and tajines. Definitely an acquired taste—Smen has an earthy pungency.

900g (1lb 14oz) unsalted butter	½ cup (125ml/4fl oz) water
2 tablespoons coarse salt	2 tablespoons dried oregano leaves

Bring the butter to room temperature. Break up into small pieces, place onto a large platter and sprinkle with 1 tablespoon of the salt. Knead the salt into the butter (as you would knead bread). Add the remaining salt and continue to knead until all the salt is absorbed into the butter.

Put the butter into the bottom of a sterilised 1½L (48fl oz) capacity, wide mouth preserving jar, pressing down with your hands to remove any air pockets. Pour the water over the butter.

Place the oregano leaves into a piece of dry, clean cloth—wrap and tie the top. Put the oregano into the water layer at the top of the jar, put lid on and seal the jar. Store in a cool, dark place (do not refrigerate). Wait at least 2 weeks before using.

Ras el Hanout

Makes about 2 tablespoons

Ras el Hanout, which translates literally as 'Head of the Shop', originated in the Meghribi villages of North Africa. It is a complex and distinctive mix of about 20–27 spices and herbs, the quantities of which vary according to the maker. Specific quantities are a much guarded secret from one spice shop to the next, and blending is considered an art.
Ras el Hanout is used with poultry, meat, game, rice and couscous. It can be found already mixed in specialty stores. If you are unable to find it, here is a simple recipe for you to make your own.

1½ teaspoons black peppercorns	¼ teaspoon cardamom seeds
1 teaspoon ground ginger	¼ teaspoon hot paprika
1 teaspoon cumin seeds	4 whole cloves
1 teaspoon coriander seeds	¼ teaspoon ground turmeric
1 teaspoon ground cinnamon	¼ teaspoon sea salt
¼ teaspoon ground nutmeg	¼ teaspoon ground allspice

Grind all the ingredients together with a mortar and pestle. Use as instructed in recipes.

Sweet and Sour Glaze

Makes about 2 cups

½ cup (125ml/4fl oz) white vinegar	1 teaspoon hot paprika
1 cup (250ml/8fl oz) olive oil	1 clove garlic, crushed
1 cup (125g/4oz) icing (confectioners') sugar	1 bunch flat leaf parsley, chopped
2 tablespoons sweet paprika	1 teaspoon salt

Whisk all ingredients well together, use as a glaze for freshly steamed vegetables, or to glaze citrus fruit for salads.

moroccan black dried olives with preserved lemon

Makes 500g (1lb)

500g (1lb) Moroccan Dried Black Olives (see page 39)
1 Preserved Lemon (see page 29)

1 teaspoon dried oregano
½ teaspoon hot paprika
2 tablespoons olive oil

Soak the olives in cold water overnight to remove excess salt, drain and allow to dry.

Squeeze the juice of the Preserved Lemon into a bowl. Dice the peel of the Preserved Lemon and add to the bowl along with the oregano, paprika and olive oil. Mix well, add the olives and stir to coat. Store in a sterilised airtight jar in the refrigerator. These will keep indefinitely. Serve as an appetiser, or add to your favourite salads.

za'atar

Makes about 4½ tablespoons

This spice blend is widely used in North Africa, also Jordan, Israel, Greece and Turkey. Usually sprinkled onto food as a seasoning, Za'atar is also used in recipes as a spice, and is often served with bread and olive oil as a breakfast dish. Za'atar can be purchased ready mixed at some Middle Eastern food stores, or you can make your own with this simple recipe.

2 tablespoons sesame seeds
1 tablespoon dried thyme

2 teaspoons dried oregano
1 tablespoon ground sumac

Dry roast the sesame seeds over a gentle heat in a frying pan, until they are just coloured. Cool the sesame seeds, then grind with a mortar and pestle with the other herbs to a fine powder. Store in a sealed jar.

Semi-dried Tomato and
Preserved Lemon Dressing

Anchovy and
Caper Dressing

Sweet and
Sour Glaze

Summer
Salad
Dressing

Basic Moroccan
Salad Dressing

Yoghurt, Mint and Sultana Dressing

Basic Moroccan Salad Dressing

Makes about 2 cups

Moroccans use great quantities of delicious fruity olive oil in their cooking and in dressings for salads. Also used in abundance are garlic, flat leaf parsley, coriander (cilantro), hot and sweet paprika, and cumin. This basic salad dressing combines a few of these Moroccan favourites in a simple to make and easy to use dressing, suitable for drizzling on all your favourite salads.

½ cup (125ml/4fl oz) white wine vinegar or lemon juice
1 cup (250ml/8fl oz) olive oil
6 garlic cloves, finely chopped
1 teaspoon sweet paprika

¼ teaspoon hot paprika
salt and freshly ground black pepper, to taste
4 tablespoons chopped flat leaf parsley
4 tablespoons chopped coriander

Whisk all the ingredients together in a bowl, leave to stand for about 15 minutes before using to allow the flavours to blend. Drizzle over your favourite salads. Keep refrigerated for up to 2 weeks.

Anchovy and Caper Dressing

Makes about 2 cups

8 anchovy fillets
1 egg, boiled (not too hard)
2 tablespoons capers, drained
½ cup (80g/2½oz) pickled cocktail onions

½ cup (125ml/4fl oz) balsamic vinegar
1 cup (250ml/8fl oz) olive oil
freshly ground black pepper, to taste

Place all ingredients except the oil into a food processor. Start processing, adding the olive oil gradually, until all the oil is used and the dressing is thick and creamy. Serve with seafood or egg salads.

soups and entrées

moroccan sardines

Serves 4

1 onion, diced	1 tablespoon sweet paprika
2 garlic cloves, chopped	juice of ½ lemon
1 small hot red chilli, chopped	salt and freshly ground black pepper to taste
1 tablespoon chopped flat leaf parsley	16 fresh sardine fillets
1 tablespoon chopped coriander (cilantro)	plain (all purpose) flour, for coating
½ tablespoon ground cumin	2 tablespoons olive oil
1 tablespoon chopped fresh ginger	Tomato Charmoula Sauce (see page 38), to serve
½ teaspoon saffron threads	

Blend the onion, garlic, chilli, herbs, spices and lemon juice in blender until all ingredients are combined. Season with salt and pepper.

Spread some of the mixture onto 1 sardine fillet and join with another, like a sandwich. Repeat with remaining sardines.

Coat the joined sardines lightly in flour, and fry in olive oil in a hot pan for about 1 minute each side, until golden brown.

Serve with Tomato Charmoula Sauce.

Harira Soup

Serves 6–8

This traditional soup is eaten to break the fast during the month of Ramadan. This is a vegetarian version of Harira soup, but those who like meat can add lamb, chicken or beef. In Morocco Harira soup is served with a bowl of fresh dates, and although this may seem unusual, the combination is delicious.

200g (7oz) chickpeas
½ cup (125ml/4fl oz) olive oil
1 tablespoon chopped fresh ginger
4 garlic cloves, crushed
2 onions, diced
2 bay leaves
2 sticks celery, chopped
1L (32fl oz) vegetable stock
200g (7oz) dried brown lentils
pinch saffron threads
1 tablespoon saffron colouring
1 tablespoon sweet paprika
½ red chilli, finely chopped

1 tablespoon ground cumin
salt and pepper to taste
2 cups (500ml/16fl oz) water
5 tablespoons plain (all purpose) flour
juice of 1 lemon
2 x 400g (14oz) cans crushed canned tomatoes
1 bunch flat leaf parsley, chopped
1 bunch coriander (cilantro), chopped
150g (5oz) vermicelli pasta, broken up
extra coriander (cilantro), to garnish
croutons or hot crusty bread, to serve
fresh dates, to serve

Soak the chickpeas in a large bowl of water overnight. Heat the olive oil in a large pot, and fry the ginger, garlic, onions, bay leaves and celery until the onion softens. Add 2 cups of the stock and the chickpeas, and bring to the boil. Reduce the heat slightly and simmer for 20 minutes.

Add the lentils, saffron threads and colouring, sweet paprika, chilli, cumin, salt and pepper. Cover with remaining stock, bring to the boil and simmer for a further 5 minutes.

In a glass or stainless steel bowl, gradually mix the water into the flour. Add the lemon juice and tomatoes. Place the bowl over the steaming pot, stirring constantly until the mixture thickens.

Add the parsley and coriander to the bowl, then add the mixture to the soup, stirring constantly. Simmer for 30 minutes, stirring occasionally.

Add vermicelli and simmer for a further 5 minutes. Garnish with coriander and serve with croutons or hot crusty bread. Serves dates on the side.

Breathless Briouats

Serves 4

1.4kg (2lb 14oz) chicken
1 tablespoon olive oil
2 bay leaves
1 cinnamon stick
salt and freshly ground pepper, to taste
1 tablespoon chopped flat leaf parsley
½ teaspoon saffron threads
1 tablespoon chopped fresh ginger
1L (32fl oz) water
16 sheets spring roll pastry
vegetable oil, for deep frying
orange segments, sesame seeds
and mint leaves, to garnish

Filling

2 white onions, diced
1 cup (90g/3oz) flaked almonds, or pine nuts
2 tablespoons orange blossom water
1 egg yolk, lightly whisked

Sauce

2 tablespoons orange blossom water
4 tablespoons caster sugar

Cut the chicken into quarters. Heat the oil in a large pot and brown the chicken. Add the bay leaves, cinnamon stick, salt and pepper, parsley, saffron and ginger. Cover with water and simmer for about 30 minutes, until the chicken is cooked.

Remove the chicken and pull the meat from the bones. Place the bones back into the pot, and reduce the stock until ⅓ is remaining. Set aside for the sauce. Chop the chicken finely.

To make the filling, fry the onion in about 2 tablespoons of the reduced stock until soft, add the almonds and orange blossom water. Add the onion mixture to the chopped chicken and mix well to combine.

To make the sauce, remove the bones from the stock. Bring slowly to the boil, add the orange blossom water and sugar. Simmer until thickened slightly.

Place 2 tablespoons of the chicken mixture onto each pastry square, fold into a cigar shape and seal the edges neatly with egg yolk. Deep fry for about 4 minutes, until golden brown. Lift out and drain for a couple of minutes, then deep fry for 1 more minute. This makes them extra crisp. Drain on absorbent paper.

Pour the sauce onto serving plates and arrange the briouats on top. Garnish with orange segments, sesame seeds and mint leaves. Serve immediately.

lentil and vegetable soup

Serves 8

500g (1lb) dried brown lentils
½ cup (125ml/4fl oz) extra virgin olive oil
4 white onions, chopped
8 large garlic cloves, finely chopped
3 sticks celery, sliced
4 ripe tomatoes, peeled and chopped
8 cups (2L/64fl oz) water

3 bay leaves
½ cup chopped coriander (cilantro) leaves
salt and freshly ground black pepper, to taste
1 red chilli, seeded and sliced
3 tablespoons tomato paste (tomato concentrate)
2 carrots, diced
crusty bread, to serve

Rinse the lentils in cold water, drain and set aside. In a large, heavy-based saucepan, heat the olive oil over a moderate heat and fry the onions, garlic and celery for about 5 minutes, until soft and golden.

Add the tomatoes, water, bay leaves and coriander (cilantro), and season with salt and pepper to taste. Bring to the boil, add the chilli, lentils, tomato paste and carrots. Stir well, reduce the heat and simmer for 30–45 mins or until the lentils are tender. Add more water if necessary. Serve with crusty bread. Store in the refrigerator for up to 1 week.

Note: You can also add broccoli, cauliflower, beans or other vegetables of your choice.

minted lamb and mushroom kebabs

Serves 4

1 cup (35g/1¼oz) mint leaves
1 Preserved Lemon (see page 29), flesh only
400g (13oz) boneless lean lamb fillet or steaks, cut into 2cm (¾in) cubes
32 button mushrooms
½ cup sliced spring onions (scallions)

freshly ground black pepper to taste
Couscous, Asparagus and Chickpea (Garbanzo) Salad (see page 164), to serve
Yoghurt, Mint and Sultana Dressing (see page 26), to serve
sweet paprika, to garnish

Combine the mint and Preserved Lemon flesh in a food processor or blender and process to a paste. Place the diced lamb, mushrooms and spring onions (scallions) into a shallow dish, spoon the mint paste over, season with pepper and toss gently to combine. Cover and refrigerate for about 20 minutes.

Thread the meat and mushrooms onto skewers. Reserve the marinade. Cook the kebabs on a preheated hot barbecue or in a char grill pan over high heat, turning and brushing with the reserved marinade frequently for 8–10 minutes or until cooked.

Serve hot on a bed of Couscous, Asparagus and Chickpea (Garbanzo) Salad, drizzled with Yoghurt, Mint and Sultana Dressing. Garnish with a dusting of sweet paprika.

chicken wishbone wings

Serves 4

12 chicken wings

1 cup (250ml/8fl oz) tomato sauce (ketchup)

2 onions, diced

4 garlic cloves, crushed

1 tablespoon English mustard

1 tablespoon chopped thyme

1 tablespoon chilli powder

2 tablespoons tandoori paste

2 teaspoons grated fresh ginger

½ teaspoon saffron threads

2 tablespoons Worcestershire sauce

1 tablespoon lemon juice

pinch salt

1 cup (250g/8oz) natural yoghurt

½ cup (125ml/4fl oz) coconut milk

150g (5oz) blue cheese

extra yoghurt, to serve

Cut the tips from the chicken wings and discard. Cut wings at the join.

Place the tomato sauce, onions, garlic, mustard, thyme, chilli powder, tandoori paste, ginger, saffron threads, Worcestershire sauce, lemon juice and salt in a shallow dish and mix well.

Add the chicken wings, and coat in the marinade. Marinate for around 20 minutes before stirring through the yoghurt, then refrigerate overnight.

Preheat the oven to 180°C (350°F/Gas 4). Take the chicken wings out of the marinade, and arrange in a single layer on an oven tray. Roast for about 30 minutes, until golden brown.

Place the marinade into a frying pan. Bring just to the boil, add the coconut milk and blue cheese. Stir over low heat until the blue cheese melts and the sauce is smooth.

To serve, place the dipping sauce into a bowl and dollop a little extra yoghurt in the centre. Arrange the chicken wings on a plate with the bowl in the centre.

liver with Eggplant (aubergine)

Serves 4

1 eggplant (aubergine)	1 teaspoon black pepper
1 tablespoon salt	1 tablespoon ground cumin
1 cup (250ml/8fl oz) milk	2 garlic cloves, chopped
½ cup (75g/2¼oz) plain flour	½ cup (125ml/4fl oz) olive oil
olive oil, to fry	200g (7oz) liver (lamb's fry)
1 Preserved Lemon, (see page 29), flesh only	1 teaspoon salt, extra
1 tablespoon chopped basil	sprigs of dill, to garnish

Cut the eggplant (aubergine) lengthways into thin slices. Spread out in a single layer, and sprinkle with salt. Leave to stand for 30 minutes to draw out any bitterness. Rinse and pat dry. Soak in milk for 2 minutes, then coat lightly with flour to seal. Fry slices in olive oil until golden brown. Set aside to cool.

In a bowl, mix the Preserved Lemon, basil, black pepper, half the cumin, garlic and olive oil. Coat the cooked eggplant strips in this mixture and leave to marinate until needed.

Sprinkle the liver with combined remaining cumin and the extra salt. Barbecue the whole liver for about 5 minutes each side, taking care not to overcook.

Cut the liver into thin slices, wrap in eggplant (aubergine) strips and secure with toothpicks if you wish. Garnish with a sprig of dill and serve as a finger food.

Note: Choose a long, thin shaped eggplant, to get the right size slices for this dish.

potato and leek soup

Serves 4

½ teaspoon black peppercorns
½ teaspoon coriander seeds
½ teaspoon cumin seeds
2 tablespoons olive oil
2 garlic cloves, crushed
3 leeks, sliced (see Note)
5 cups (1.25L/40fl oz) chicken stock
8 medium to large potatoes, peeled

2 bay leaves
½ teaspoon salt
2 cups (500ml/16fl oz) water
1–3 tablespoons sour cream, optional
deep fried leeks, to garnish, optional
extra sour cream to garnish
warm crusty bread, to serve

Preheat the oven to 190°C (375°F/Gas 5). Place the peppercorns, coriander and cumin seeds onto an oven tray and dry roast for about 5 minutes, until fragrant. Crush with a mortar and pestle.

Heat the olive oil in a large saucepan over a medium heat. Add the crushed seeds and garlic, and fry for 2 minutes to release the flavours. Add the sliced leeks and fry for a further 2 minutes before adding the stock.

Add the potatoes, bay leaves and salt. Bring to the boil, reduce heat and simmer partially covered for about 1 hour, adding water if necessary, until the potatoes are very tender. Remove from the heat. Drain the potatoes and leeks, reserving the liquid. Discard the bay leaves.

Using a food processor, blender or even a potato masher, blend potatoes and leeks together adding enough of the liquid for the consistency you prefer. Add sour cream if you like, and salt and pepper to taste.

This is great served with fresh warm crusty bread. To garnish, add a spoonful of sour cream and sprinkle with deep fried leeks.

This soup will freeze for about 3 months. Defrost at room temperature, and add a little milk when reheating, if necessary.

Note: The best way to slice leeks is to chop the roots and tops off, and cut lengthwise in half. This will allow you to wash the leek properly between the layers. Discard any bad leaves, and slice into semicircles.

Kefta Briouats

Makes 16

2 brown onions	1 teaspoon white pepper
1 tablespoon olive oil	500g (1lb) lean minced (ground) beef
20g (⅔oz) butter	4 eggs
1 teaspoon salt	16 sheets spring roll pastry
2 tablespoons chopped flat leaf parsley	30g (1oz) butter, melted
2 tablespoons chopped coriander (cilantro)	1 egg yolk
1 tablespoon sweet paprika	vegetable oil, for deep frying

Peel and finely dice the onions, fry in olive oil and butter until soft. Add the salt, parsley, coriander (cilantro), paprika, pepper and beef. Cook until well browned, breaking up any lumps with a wooden spoon.

Add the eggs one at a time—breaking in whole and mixing through the mince. This process should take around 15 minutes. Take off the heat and allow to cool.

Lay out the pastry sheets and brush with melted butter. Put a spoonful of beef mixture onto a corner of each sheet, and roll diagonally into a cigar shape. Fold in the edges like a parcel as you go to enclose the filling. Seal with egg yolk.

Deep fry for about 4 minutes, until golden brown. Lift out and drain for a couple of minutes, then deep fry for 1 more minute. This makes them extra crisp.

Drain on absorbent paper. Serve hot as a finger food.

Rghaif des Ferran

Makes 10

A delicious Moroccan spicy bread, similar to Turkish pide.
The dough is like a handmade filo—crispy and flaky.

Dough	Filling
500g (1lb) plain (all purpose) flour	1 bunch flat leaf parsley, chopped
2 teaspoons salt	½ onion, grated
2 teaspoons dried yeast	100g (3½oz) minced (ground) lamb
1 cup (250ml/8fl oz) tepid water	½ teaspoon sweet paprika
½ cup (125ml/4fl oz) vegetable oil	50g (1¾oz) ricotta cheese
	½ teaspoon ground cumin
	pinch chilli powder
	1 cup (90g/3oz) sliced button mushrooms

Preheat the oven to 180°C (350°F/Gas 4). Sift the flour onto a board or bench top, add the salt and yeast. Add the water mixing briskly as you go, until a firm dough is formed. It should be a little softer than bread dough, but very elastic and easy to handle. Form into 20 balls about the size of an apricot, and place on a slightly oiled surface.

To make the filling, mix all the ingredients together in a bowl.

Take the first dough ball and flatten and stretch using oiled fingertips, press out all sides to form a square, making it pastry thin. Keep the dough and hands oily so the dough slips easily.

Place a spoonful of filling into the middle of the dough.

Spread out a second dough ball as thinly as the first, place the stuffed parcel bottom side up into the centre of this new pastry layer and fold the sides in again to form a double layered pastry parcel. Repeat this process to form 10 parcels. Place on a lightly oiled baking tray and cook for 30 minutes.

Eat hot as they come out of the oven. Serve with Mint Tea (see page 207).

pan Fried Herbed calamari (squid) salad

Serves 4

2 garlic cloves, crushed
½ cup (125ml/4fl oz) olive oil
I Preserved Lemon (see page 29), flesh only
I tablespoon chopped basil
I tablespoon chopped flat leaf parsley
I tablespoon chopped coriander (cilantro)
I teaspoon chopped thyme
I teaspoon finely chopped red chilli

I tablespoon sweet paprika
I teaspoon salt
500g (1lb) calamari (squid) tubes
I tablespoon olive oil, extra
mixed baby lettuce, roasted Roma tomatoes and lemon wedges, to serve
Semi-dried Tomato and Preserved Lemon Dressing (see page 35)

Preheat the oven to 200°C (400°F/Gas 6). Blend the garlic, olive oil, Preserved Lemon, basil, parsley, coriander, thyme, chilli, paprika and salt in a food processor until smooth.

Slice the calamari tubes into 1.5cm (⅝in) rings and coat well with the marinade, leave to stand for 30 minutes.

Heat the extra olive oil in a frying pan until hot. Add the calamari and saute for about 3 minutes until opaque. Place onto an oven tray and cook in the oven for a further 5 minutes.

Serve on a bed of mixed baby lettuce with roasted Roma tomatoes and lemon wedges. Drizzle with Semi-dried Tomato and Preserved Lemon Dressing.

Hassan's potato, olive and Harissa tortilla

Serves 10—12

500g (1lb) potatoes	1 tablespoon Harissa (see page 26)
½ cup (125ml/4fl oz) olive oil	4 eggs
1 large red onion, chopped	1 cup (250ml/8fl oz) cream
4 garlic cloves, crushed	3 tablespoons chopped coriander (cilantro)
1 cup (150g/5oz) frozen green peas, thawed	1 teaspoon salt
½ cup Moroccan Dried Black Olives	½ cup (125g/4oz) sour cream
(see page 39)	1 tablespoon caviar

Preheat the oven to 180°C (350°F/Gas 4). Brush a deep 30cm (12in) diameter ovenproof dish with melted butter, and line with non-stick baking paper.

Peel the potatoes, cut lengthways into quarters, then into 1cm (⅜in) slices. Reserve 1 tablespoon of the oil, and fry the potatoes in the remaining oil until crisp and browned on both sides. Drain on absorbent paper.

Heat the reserved oil in a large saucepan and fry the onion and garlic for about 1 minute. Mix in the peas, Moroccan Dried Black Olives and Harissa, take off the heat and set aside.

Lightly whisk the eggs and cream together in a bowl then stir in the coriander (cilantro) and salt.

Add the potatoes to the onion mixture in the saucepan, then add the cream mixture and stir gently together.

Pour the potato mixture into the prepared dish, and bake for 10 minutes. Reduce the heat to 160°C (325°F/Gas 3) and cook a further 10 minutes until set. Take out of the oven and stand for 30 minutes. Turn upside down onto a serving platter and cover with sour cream. Garnish with the caviar. Can be served hot or cold.

charmoula baby octopus and mussels

Serves 4

1kg (2lb) baby octopus, cleaned and cut in half lengthways
½ cup Charmoula Marinade (see page 32)
1 tablespoon Harissa (see page 26)
400g (14oz) can crushed tomatoes
½ cup Moroccan Dried Black Olives (see page 39)

1kg (2lb) mussels, cleaned, opened, and discard ½ the shell
1 bunch fresh coriander (cilantro), chopped
grilled Roma tomatoes, lemon wedges and basil leaves, to garnish

Preheat the oven to 120°C (250°F/Gas 1).

Marinate the octopus in Charmoula Marinade for 30 minutes.

Heat a large frying pan until very hot and fry the octopus for about 5 minutes, until pink and tender. Take out the octopus, cover loosely with foil and keep warm in the oven.

Add the Harissa and crushed tomatoes to the marinade left in the frying pan. Turn down the heat and simmer for 5 minutes then stir in the Moroccan Dried Black Olives. Place the mussels (shell side up) into the sauce and sprinkle all over with the coriander. Cover with a lid and steam the mussels for 3 minutes.

To serve, place the octopus in the middle of shallow serving bowls. Surround with the sauce, and arrange the mussels in half shells around the outside edge. Garnish with grilled Roma tomatoes, lemon wedges and basil leaves.

OOA oysters

Serves 4

2 fresh bird's eye chillies	½ cup (125ml/4fl oz) extra virgin olive oil
4 tablespoons chopped fresh coriander (cilantro)	4 dozen oysters, on the half shell
juice of 3 limes	4 tablespoons red caviar
3 garlic cloves, crushed	lime wedges, to serve
½ teaspoon salt	

Cut the chillies in half and discard the seeds. Chop the flesh and combine in a bowl with the coriander (cilantro). Add the lime juice, garlic, salt and olive oil and mix well together. Spoon onto each of the oysters and top with a little caviar. Serve with lime wedges.

Harsha

Makes 16

A very versatile flat bread, Harsha can be used with many variations of savoury toppings. You may like to use them as mini pizza bases, top them with salsa, use as a bread with dips or simply just dip in olive oil with a bit of balsamic vinegar.

200g (7oz) butter, cubed	2 teaspoons dried yeast
500g (1lb) fine semolina	1 cup (250ml/8fl oz) milk
¼ teaspoon salt	100g (3½oz) coarse semolina
1 tablespoon sugar	vegetable oil, to cook

Using your fingertips, rub the butter into the fine semolina. Add the salt, sugar, yeast and milk, mix to make a dough. Knead the dough well using the palms of your hands.

Divide the dough into 16 balls. Sprinkle coarse semolina onto a flat surface. Knead each ball and flatten to a round disc, about 1cm (⅜in) thick, sprinkling more coarse semolina on top.

Grease a non-stick fry pan with vegetable oil. Heat the pan over high heat, and fry the Harsha until golden brown on both sides, using a spatula to flatten out gently during cooking. Serve hot with your choice of topping.

Opposite: OOA oysters

Gazpacho

Serves 6

This soup is of Spanish origin, its popularity spreading across the Straits of Gibraltar, making it a favourite summer soup in Morocco. It may be blended until smooth, or you may prefer to retain the crunch of fresh vegetables by adding them coarsely chopped.

2kg (4lb) large ripe tomatoes	2 tablespoons olive oil
1 medium onion, finely diced	1 tablespoon vegetable oil
1 large carrot, finely diced	2 garlic cloves, crushed
1 green capsicum (bell pepper), finely diced	salt and freshly ground black pepper, to taste
2 sticks celery, finely diced	juice of ½ lemon
1 Lebanese cucumber, seeded and finely diced	Harsha (see page 72), to serve
½ bunch flat leaf parsley, chopped	

Peel and coarsely chop the tomatoes. Put aside a little of the diced vegetables to serve on the side of the soup.

Place the tomatoes and remaining diced vegetables, parsley, both oils, garlic, salt and pepper into a blender 1 cup at a time and blend until smooth. Pour into a glass bowl and refrigerate until chilled. Stir in the lemon juice.

To serve, pour into bowls, and present a bowl of diced vegetables on the side. Serve with freshly made Harsha.

Roasted Roma Tomatoes with Grilled Goat's Cheese

Serves 4

An exotic modern Moroccan entree.

4 medium ripe Roma tomatoes	vegetable oil, to fry
1 tablespoon Harissa (see page 26)	2 cups Spinach Salad with Preserved Lemon
8cm (3in) log goat cheese	(see page 184)
1 egg, lightly beaten	½ cup Semi-dried Tomato and Preserved Lemon
2 tablespoons Za'atar (see page 43)	Dressing (see page 35)

Preheat the oven to 140°C (275°F/Gas 1–2). Cut each tomato in half lengthways and remove seeds. Toss in Harissa, place into a shallow baking dish and roast for 20 minutes. Set aside to cool.

Cut the goat cheese into 4 slices. Dip in the egg, and roll in the Za'atar until evenly coated. Barbecue or pan fry in vegetable oil for 5 minutes each side.

To serve, place ½ cup Spinach Salad with Preserved Lemon in the centre of each plate, top with goat cheese. Place 2 roasted tomatoes on top of each round of cheese and drizzle with Semi-dried Tomato and Preserved Lemon Dressing.

tajines

moroccan meatball tajine

Serves 4

Tomato Sauce

2 tablespoons olive oil
1 cup Charmoula Marinade (see page 32)
2 x 400g (14oz) cans crushed tomatoes
250g (8oz) frozen green peas, thawed

Meatballs

½ cup (50g/1¾oz) dried breadcrumbs
½ cup (125ml/4fl oz) milk
1 teaspoon ground cumin
1 teaspoon ground paprika
1 teaspoon chilli powder
1 tablespoon chopped flat leaf parsley
1 tablespoon chopped coriander (cilantro)
1 egg
2 tablespoons olive oil
1 kg (2lb) minced (ground) beef
salt and pepper, to taste

2 tablespoons chopped flat leaf parsley
1 egg, extra, to serve

For the Tomato Sauce, heat the olive oil in a saucepan and fry the Charmoula Marinade for about 5 minutes, until softened. Add the tomatoes and simmer on low heat for 20 minutes. While the sauce is simmering, prepare the meatballs.

Preheat the oven to 190°C (375°F/Gas 5). To make the meatballs, soak the breadcrumbs in the milk until soft, then use your hands to mix with the remaining ingredients until well combined. Roll into balls the size of golf balls. Arrange in a single layer in a shallow ovenproof dish, and bake for 10 minutes to seal and partially cook.

Add the peas to the tomato sauce and simmer for 5 minutes. Add the meatballs, coat them in sauce and simmer for a further 5 minutes

Place a tajine or heavy-based flameproof dish over low heat. Place meatballs around the outside and sprinkle with parsley. Pour the sauce with peas into the middle. Break a raw egg into the middle of the dish and cover. Cook gently for a few minutes to allow the steam to partly poach the egg. Serve immediately.

sweet lamb tajine

Serves 4

3 white onions
2 tablespoons sweet paprika
1 teaspoon saffron threads
1 tablespoon chopped ginger
3 bay leaves
salt and freshly ground black pepper, to taste
½ cup (125ml/4fl oz) olive oil
8 lamb forequarter (or neck) chops

2 cups (500ml/16fl oz) water
juice of 2 oranges
½ cup (125ml/4fl oz) honey
1 tablespoon ground cinnamon
8 prunes, pitted
½ cup (75g/2¼oz) roast blanched almonds
sesame seeds, to garnish
2 hard boiled eggs, quartered

Chop one of the onions, and cut the other two into rings. Combine the chopped onion with the paprika, saffron, ginger, bay leaves, salt and pepper and the olive oil. Cut the chops in half and coat with this mixture. Marinate for 4 hours, or overnight if possible.

Brown chops in a heavy-based pan for 10 minutes on medium heat, add water and bring to the boil. Simmer for 20 minutes, then add the other 2 onions, orange juice, honey and cinnamon. Simmer a further 15 minutes. Stand for 15 minutes then transfer the meat to a tajine. Pour the sweet onion sauce from the pot over the top and garnish with prunes, almonds, sesame seeds and boiled eggs. Serve immediately.

chicken tajine with preserved lemon and olives

Serves 2

If you use a free range chicken for this recipe, you will only need
to marinate for 30 minutes, rather than overnight.

1.2 kg (2lb 7oz) chicken	2 brown onions, halved and finely sliced
½ cup Charmoula Marinade (see page 32)	1 tomato, peeled, seeded and chopped
4 tablespoons peanut oil	1 bunch flat leaf parsley, chopped
½ teaspoon salt	1 bunch coriander (cilantro), chopped
½ teaspoon saffron threads	2 large potatoes, cut into wedges
½ teaspoon freshly ground black pepper	2 cups (500ml/16fl oz) water
½ teaspoon ground cumin	150g (5oz) green olives
½ teaspoon ground ginger	1 Preserved Lemon (see page 29), cut into
1 cinnamon stick	6 segments
4 garlic cloves, crushed	coriander (cilantro) leaves, to garnish

Wash and dry the chicken and cut into quarters. Rub all over with Charmoula Marinade, refrigerate overnight.

In a large heavy-based saucepan or flameproof casserole dish, heat the peanut oil and brown the chicken. Add the salt, saffron, pepper, cumin, ginger, cinnamon stick, garlic and onion and cook for 10 minutes, turning the chicken occasionally.

Add the tomato, parsley, coriander (cilantro), potatoes and water. Bring to the boil, reduce the heat and simmer, covered, for 45 minutes. When the chicken is cooked, remove from the saucepan and place onto a tajine or serving dish. Reduce the stock for 5 minutes then add the olives and Preserved Lemon. To serve, place the potatoes around the chicken, cover with the sauce and garnish with fresh coriander (cilantro).

HASSAN'S FISH TAJINE

Serves 4

4 x 5cm (2in) thick Blue-eye cod fillets (approx 1kg/2lb) or turbot or halibut
2 cups Tomato Charmoula Sauce (see page 38)
1 stick celery
1 carrot
2 potatoes
1 small red capsicum (bell pepper)

1 small green capsicum (bell pepper)
2 tablespoons tomato paste (tomato concentrate)
2 cups (500ml/16fl oz) fish stock
½ cup (90g/3oz) Kalamata olives
1 Preserved Lemon (see page 29), cut into wedges
2 Roma tomatoes, halved and roasted
2 tablespoons chopped coriander (cilantro)

Marinate the fish in the Tomato Charmoula Sauce for 2 hours.

Split the celery stick in half lengthwise and place slices parallel to each other in the bottom of a tajine or large flameproof casserole dish (this prevents the fish burning on the bottom).

Arrange the fish over the celery.

Slice the carrot diagonally in 1cm (⅜in) thick slices. Peel and slice the potatoes double the thickness of the carrot. Discard the seeds and membrane from the capsicums (bell peppers) and slice the flesh to double the thickness of the potato (as each of the vegetables take different periods of time to cook, preparing them in this way prevents any of them being overcooked).

Alternate the carrot and potato slices around the outer edge of the dish on top of the fish. Place the capsicums (bell peppers), alternating red and green, on top of the whole dish.

Mix the remaining Tomato Charmoula Sauce with the tomato paste and fish stock and whisk until well combined. Pour over the vegetables and fish, and top with the olives and Preserved Lemon wedges.

Cover the tajine or casserole dish with a lid and simmer over a low heat for 45 minutes.

Serve the fish tajine directly to the table, garnished with the tomatoes and sprinkled with fresh coriander (cilantro).

meat and poultry

lamb couscous with vegetables

Serves 4

8 lamb forequarter (or neck) chops
1 cup Charmoula Marinade (see page 32)
750g (1½lb) couscous
salt, to taste
½ teaspoon saffron threads
1 brown onion, halved and finely sliced
3 ripe tomatoes, chopped
3 carrots, cut lengthways into quarters

4 zucchini, cut lengthways into quarters
3 parsnips, cut lengthways into quarters
½ butternut pumpkin (butternut squash), cut into cubes
2 tablespoons olive oil
Sweet Chickpeas (see page 160)
Harissa (see page 26)

Marinate the lamb in the Charmoula Marinade for at least 4 hours, or overnight if possible.

Place the couscous into a bowl, and cover with water. Add salt and the saffron threads. Soak for 10 minutes.

Lightly fry the marinated lamb to seal and brown slightly. Place it into the bottom of a couscoussier, cover with water and gently bring to the boil. Place the next level of steamer (a fine-holed tray for the couscous) over the boiling lamb. Drain the couscous and place evenly into the second level of steamer. Steam uncovered for about 15 minutes, or until steam begins to come through the couscous.

Add the onion, tomatoes and carrots (plus extra water if required) to the lamb, and boil for 10 minutes until carrots are partly cooked. Add the zucchini (courgette), parsnips and pumpkin.

While this is cooking, remove the couscous from the steamer and place into a bowl. Work the grain well with your fingers to separate. Add the oil (to seal the grain) and 1 cup (250ml/8fl oz) of cold water. Return to the steamer and cook again until the steam begins to come through the couscous. (These extra preparations may seem a little laborious but ensures that the couscous is fluffy, juicy and correctly cooked…it makes all the difference!!)

To serve, place couscous around the outside of a heated serving platter, place the lamb pieces in the centre and decorate the outside with the vegetables. Garnish with Sweet Chickpeas and extra boullion from the lamb and vegetables.

Extra bouillon can also be further seasoned with spices or Harissa and served separately for those guests who prefer a little more spice.

Harissa Baked chicken

Serves 4

4 chicken breast fillets
2–3 teaspoons Harissa (see page 26)
2 tablespoons chopped coriander (cilantro)
1 tablespoon finely chopped Preserved Lemon
(see page 29)
16 filo pastry sheets
50g (1¾oz) butter, melted

4 artichoke hearts, sliced
4 Roma tomatoes, sliced
1 egg yolk
1 tablespoon toasted cumin seeds
extra toasted cumin seeds and strips of Preserved
Lemon rind, to serve

Preheat the oven to 150°C (300°F/Gas 2). Make a pocket in the side of each chicken breast. Spread the inside of the chicken with Harissa then stuff with coriander (cilantro) and Preserved Lemon.

Brush a filo sheet with melted butter, layer a second on top, brush again and repeat with 3rd and 4th sheets until you have a stack of four, repeat until you have 4 stacks of pastry.

Place artichoke and tomato slices with cumin seeds in a pile in the centre of each pastry stack. Top the vegetables with a chicken breast. Fold tightly like a parcel and seal by brushing with egg yolk. Turn upside down so the artichoke and tomato side faces up and place on a baking tray. Bake for 40 minutes, until chicken is cooked.

Garnish with the extra toasted cumin seeds and strips of Preserved Lemon rind.

B'stilla

Serves 4–6

chicken

1.4kg (2lb 14oz) whole chicken
2 tablespoons olive oil
1 brown onion, diced
1 clove garlic, crushed
1 tablespoon grated ginger
1 teaspoon saffron threads
2 bay leaves
1 Preserved Lemon (see page 29)
3 cups (750ml/24fl oz) water
salt and freshly ground black pepper, to taste

creamy eggs

6 eggs, lightly beaten
½ bunch coriander (cilantro), chopped
½ cup (125ml/4fl oz) orange blossom water

Glazed onion

½ cup (125ml/4fl oz) orange blossom water
1 brown onion, halved and finely sliced
1 cup (125g/4oz) icing (confectioners') sugar
1 cup (90g/3oz) toasted flaked almonds
1 tablespoon ground cinnamon

100g (3½oz) butter
1 tablespoon orange blossom water
13 sheets filo pastry
2 tablespoons icing (confectioners') sugar, to dust
2 tablespoons ground cinnamon
orange segments and strawberries, to garnish

Cut the chicken into quarters. Heat the olive oil in a large saucepan, add the onion, garlic and ginger, fry for a minute then add the saffron, bay leaves and Preserved Lemon. Fry for about 3 minutes, until softened slightly.

Add the chicken and cover with water. Season with salt and pepper and simmer for about 20 minutes, until cooked. Remove the chicken from the pan. Allow to cool, then pull the meat off the bones and slice it into strips.

Boil the sauce until reduced by half. Take out half and reserve for later.

To make the creamy eggs, add the eggs, coriander (cilantro) and orange blossom water to the remaining sauce in the saucepan. Stir over low heat until creamy, taking care not to overcook. Remove from the heat and set aside.

For the glazed onion, place the reserved sauce and the orange blossom water into a frying pan and bring to the boil. Reduce the heat and simmer for 10 minutes, until reduced further. Add the onion and half of the icing (confectioners') sugar (keep the rest to dust the top), and simmer for 20 minutes. Add the almonds, stir through, sprinkle with cinnamon and set aside.

Preheat the oven to 180°C (350°F/Gas 4). Melt the butter and combine with the orange blossom water. Brush two medium pizza trays with some of the orange butter. Layer 9 sheets of filo pastry in a fan pattern covering the tray and overhanging the sides. Fold another sheet in half and place in the centre. Spoon on the glazed onion mixture, fold over 3 sheets of the overhanging filo to cover, place another folded sheet in the centre and brush with orange butter.

Spoon on the creamy eggs to make another layer. Fold over 3 more sheets of overhanging filo, place another folded sheet in the centre and brush with orange butter.

Add the chicken to make another layer and cover with folded remaining filo sheets. Fold over remaining 3 sheets of overhanging filo, brush with orange butter.

Bake in the oven until the pastry has browned on the top. Turn onto the other tray, brush with orange butter and cook to brown the underside.

Transfer to a serving tray and dust with the remaining icing sugar, then form a lattice pattern with the ground cinnamon. Serve garnished with orange segments and strawberries placed in the centre.

marrakesh express
lamb brochettes

Serves 4

1 onion, diced	3 tablespoons extra virgin olive oil
1 tablespoon ground cumin	½ tablespoon chopped coriander (cilantro)
1 garlic clove, chopped	juice of ½ lemon
salt and pepper, to taste	500g (1lb) lamb backstrap (boneless loin)
1 tablespoon chopped flat leaf parsley	Tomato Charmoula Sauce (see page 38), to serve

Mix the onion, cumin, garlic, salt and pepper, parsley, olive oil, coriander (cilantro) and lemon juice together in a bowl. Leave to sit for around 5 minutes for the flavours to merge.

Cut the lamb into bite-sized cubes, and mix with the marinade.

Cover and allow to marinate for at least 2 hours, or overnight if possible.

Thread the lamb onto wooden or metal skewers. Grill, barbecue or pan fry for about 2 minutes each side, until cooked through. Serve with Tomato Charmoula Sauce.

Hint: Lightly coat the skewers with olive oil prior to threading on lamb.
This allows the meat to be removed easily after cooking.

Kefta

Serves 4

1 kg (2lb) minced (ground) beef	1 tablespoon ground coriander
4 garlic cloves, crushed	1 tablespoon ground cumin
1 brown onion, grated	½ bunch flat leaf parsley, finely chopped
1 tablespoon finely chopped red chilli	juice of ½ lemon
1 tablespoon ground turmeric	Moroccan Dried Black Olives (see page 39) and
2 tablespoons sweet paprika	cubed feta, to serve
1 teaspoon ground black pepper	Tomato Charmoula Sauce (see page 38), to serve

Place the beef, garlic, onion, chilli, spices, parsley and lemon juice into a bowl. Use your hands to mix together until well combined. Form into sausage shapes or meatballs, or wrap around skewers.

Grill, barbecue or pan fry the Kefta, being careful not to overcook (the time required will depend on how thick your sausages or how round the meatballs). Serve on a bed of couscous, garnished with Moroccan Dried Black Olives and cubed feta, with Tomato Charmoula Sauce on the side.

Da Laa' Lamb Cutlets

Serves 4

2 tablespoons olive oil

1 teaspoon grated ginger

2 bay leaves

1 cinnamon stick

3 white onions, sliced into rings

pinch saffron threads

salt and freshly ground black pepper, to taste

½ cup (110g/3¾oz) sugar

½ cup (125ml/4fl oz) honey

½ cup (125ml/4fl oz) fresh orange juice

1 cup (180g/6oz) chopped dates

2 tablespoons Worcestershire sauce

½ Preserved Lemon (see page 29), flesh only

12 lamb cutlets

Prepared Couscous (see page 175), to serve

orange segments, to garnish

1 tablespoon sesame seeds, toasted

Heat the oil in a saucepan, add the ginger, bay leaves, cinnamon stick, onion rings, saffron, salt and pepper and fry for 5 minutes. Add the sugar and stir in the honey and orange juice and simmer for 15 minutes. Add the dates and simmer a further 5 minutes, take off the heat and keep warm.

Mix the Worcestershire sauce and Preserved Lemon flesh together, coat the cutlets well with this mixture and stand for 15 minutes. Cook the cutlets on a char grill for about 5 minutes each side until crispy on the outside but still pink on the inside.

To serve, mound couscous into the centre of serving plates. Pour the date sauce around and arrange 3 cutlets on each plate. Garnish with orange segments and sprinkle with sesame seeds.

moorish kebabs

Serves 2

prawn (shrimp)

1 tablespoon extra virgin olive oil
1 garlic clove, crushed
2 tablespoons chopped mint
salt and freshly ground black pepper, to taste
6 raw large prawns (jumbo shrimp)
½ red capsicum (bell pepper),
    cut into 3cm (1in) cubes

lamb

2 tablespoons extra virgin olive oil
2 tablespoons lemon juice
1 garlic clove, crushed
1 teaspoon ground cumin
salt and freshly ground black pepper, to taste
250g (8oz) lamb backstrap (boneless lamb
    loin), cut into 5cm (2in) cubes
8 button mushrooms

chicken

2 tablespoons olive oil
1 tablespoon lemon juice
1 teaspoon ground coriander
1 teaspoon Harissa (see page 26)
250g (8oz) chicken thigh fillets,
    cut into 5cm (2in) cubes
8 cherry tomatoes

Couscous Salad (see page 144), to serve

For the prawns, mix the oil, garlic and mint together, season with salt and pepper. Peel and devein the prawns (shrimp) leaving the heads and tails on. Pour the mixture over the prawns and marinate in the refrigerator for 30 minutes. Thread onto 2 skewers, alternating with the capsicum (bell pepper) pieces.

For the lamb, mix the oil, lemon juice, garlic, cumin and salt and pepper in a bowl. Add the lamb, coat thoroughly with marinade and leave to stand for 2 hours. Thread the lamb onto 2 skewers, alternating with the whole button mushrooms.

For the chicken, mix the oil, lemon juice, coriander and Harissa in a bowl. Add the chicken, coat well and marinate for 1 hour. Thread the chicken onto 2 skewers alternating with the cherry tomatoes.

Preheat a barbecue or char grill. Cook the prawn kebabs for 5 minutes, and the chicken and lamb for 10–15 minutes. The lamb should be brown on the outside but still pink on the inside. Turn occasionally and baste with appropriate marinade.

Serve with Couscous Salad.

steamed chicken stuffed with rice and parsley

Serves 2

½ cup (100g/3½oz) rice	1.2kg (2lb 7oz) whole chicken
500g (1lb) tomatoes, peeled, seeded and diced	1 teaspoon salt
1 bunch flat leaf parsley, chopped	2 bay leaves
1 stick celery, chopped	1 celery stick
½ Preserved Lemon (see page 29), chopped	1 carrot
½ fresh red chilli, chopped	steamed vegetables, to serve
50g (1¾oz) butter	

Wash and drain the rice, mix with the tomatoes, parsley, celery, Preserved Lemon, chilli and butter. Wash and dry the chicken and place the stuffing in the cavity. Use a small skewer to close the cavity, or stitch.

Place the stuffed chicken into the top part of a large steamer, with the bottom part containing 3–4L (24–32fl oz) of boiling water, salt, bay leaves, celery and carrot. Cover the chicken with a clean, damp cloth and place a lid on top. Steam the chicken for about 1½ hours, or until the flesh comes away from the bone. Serve with steamed vegetables.

oven bag chicken with couscous stuffing

Serves 2

stuffing

200g (7oz) couscous
1 cup (250ml/8fl oz) boiling water
½ cup (125ml/4fl oz) chicken stock
1 teaspoon olive oil
1 garlic clove, crushed
1 teaspoon dried rosemary
1 onion, diced
salt and freshly ground black pepper, to taste
¼ cup (40g/1½oz) toasted blanched almonds, finely chopped
1 cup (125g/4oz) raisins
1 tablespoon butter
pinch saffron threads

1.2kg (2lb 7oz) whole chicken
1 Preserved Lemon (see page 29), sliced
4 Kalamata olives, halved and seeded
1 tablespoon olive oil
¼ cup (60ml/2fl oz) juice from Preserved Lemons (see page 29)
1 garlic clove, crushed
salt and freshly ground black pepper, to taste

Preheat the oven to 180°C (350°F/Gas 4). To make the stuffing, place the couscous into a microwave safe bowl. Stir in the boiling water and saffron with a fork, breaking up any lumps. Microwave on high for 2 minutes. Stir in half the chicken stock, breaking up any lumps, and microwave for another 2 minutes.

Heat the oil in a frying pan and add garlic, rosemary, onion, salt and pepper. Cook over low heat until the onion softens. Stir in the almonds, then the raisins and finally the remaining chicken stock. Combine with the couscous.

Wash and clean the chicken, fill the cavity with the stuffing and secure with small skewer. Cut slits crossways along the breast and fill with slices of Preserved Lemon.

In a bowl, mix the remaining Preserved Lemon with the olives, olive oil, juice of Preserved Lemon, garlic, salt and pepper. Rub all over the outside of the chicken, place into an oven bag and seal. Bake for 1 hour and 40 minutes.

Note: For a great picnic idea, just pack the chicken in a cooler still in its bag with all the juices. Squeeze a Preserved Lemon to obtain the juice, don't just take liquid from the jar.

beef with fresh broad beans (fava beans) and artichoke

Serves 4

3 tablespoons olive oil
2 brown onions, thinly sliced
2 garlic cloves, crushed
¼ teaspoon ground ginger
salt and freshly ground black pepper, to taste
500g (1lb) beef neck (use osso bucco if not available), cut into cubes
pinch saffron threads, soaked in 2 cups (500ml/16fl oz) water

½ teaspoons sweet paprika
500g (1lb) fresh or frozen broad beans (fava beans)
500g (1lb) fresh artichokes
½ Preserved Lemon (see page 29), juice only
1 tablespoon sesame seeds

Heat the oil in a heavy-based saucepan. Fry the onions, garlic, ginger, salt and pepper until the onion is soft. Add the meat and brown all sides, then add the saffron water and paprika and bring to the boil. Reduce the heat and simmer, covered, for 30 minutes.

Add the broad beans (fava beans) and simmer for a further 15 minutes.

Remove all the outer leaves from the artichokes, then cut into quarters. Rub them all over with the Preserved Lemon juice to prevent discolouring. Add to the beef and beans and simmer partially covered for 30 minutes.

Turn off the heat, cover and leave to stand for 2 minutes.

To serve, arrange the beef in the centre of a platter. Use a slotted spoon to place beans on top and artichoke quarters around the sides. Drizzle with the sauce and sprinkle with sesame seeds.

spatchcock (poussin) with saffron apricot sauce and poppy seeds

Serves 2

	Apricot sauce
2 free range spatchcocks (poussin) (300g/10oz) each)	50g (1¾oz) poppy seeds
1 cup Charmoula Marinade (see page 32)	100g (3½oz) butter
4 tablespoons peanut oil	100g (3½oz) sugar
salt and freshly ground black pepper	1 teaspoon ground cinnamon
1 cinnamon stick	pinch saffron threads
2 cloves	500g (1lb) dried apricots, rinsed
2 cups (500ml/16fl oz) water	Saffron Risotto Cake (see page 170), to serve

Marinate the spatchcocks (poussin) in Charmoula Marinade for at least 2 hours.

Heat the oil in a large pot, and brown the spatchcocks (poussin) all over. Season with salt and pepper, add the cinnamon stick, cloves and water and simmer for 30 minutes.

When cooked, take out of the sauce and keep warm. Strain the liquid through a fine sieve and reserve.

To make the Apricot Sauce, heat a saucepan and dry fry the poppy seeds for about 30 seconds, to lightly toast. Reduce the heat and add the butter to melt. Add the sugar, cinnamon and saffron, stirring until the sugar dissolves.

Add the dried apricots and the strained liquid, and cook over a low heat, uncovered, until the sauce has a syrupy consistency. Place the spatchcock (poussin) into the sauce and coat.

Serve on Saffron Risotto Cake, with the remainder of the sauce drizzled around the plate.

veal Gibraltar (veal roll with tomato concassé)

Serves 4

The influence in creating this dish comes from the centre of the Mediterranean, with flavours
inspired by the south of Europe (Gibraltar) and the North of Africa (Morocco).
The name Gibraltar comes from the Arabic 'Jabal al Tariq' which means Tariq's Mountain.

1 eggplant (aubergine)	## tomato concassé
1 tablespoon salt	1 tablespoon olive oil
1 large red capsicum (bell pepper)	2 garlic cloves, crushed
1 cup (250ml/8fl oz) milk	8 Roma tomatoes, peeled, seeded and diced
plain (all purpose) flour, to coat	1 tablespoon butter, optional
olive oil, to fry	
4 large veal schnitzel (escalopes)	
½ cup (125g/4oz) pesto	
100g (3½oz) Camembert cheese, thinly sliced	
1 tablespoon olive oil	
1 teaspoon ground black pepper	
16 Kalamata olives	

Slice the eggplant (aubergine) lengthways into four 1cm (⅜in) thick slices, sprinkle with salt and stand
for 30 minutes to draw out any bitterness; rinse and pat dry.

Meanwhile, preheat the oven to 180°C (350°F/Gas 4). Cut the capsicum (bell pepper) into large
pieces with no seeds or membrane. Grill (broil) skin side up until blackened. Allow to cool then peel
and slice into strips.

Soak the eggplant in milk for 2 minutes, then coat lightly with flour to seal. Pan-fry in olive oil for
about 3 minutes each side, until golden brown.

Spread the 4 schnitzel (escalopes) with pesto, then layer capsicum, eggplant slices and Camembert
cheese in the centre. Roll and seal with toothpicks to prevent the filling from spilling out. Brush with
olive oil and sprinkle with pepper. Barbecue or pan-fry in hot oil to brown and seal on all sides. Place
onto a baking tray and bake for about 10 minutes to melt the cheese.

Meanwhile, make the Tomato Concassé. Heat the olive oil in a saucepan over medium heat and add the garlic, cook for 30 seconds. Stir in the tomatoes and bring to the boil. Reduce the heat and simmer for about 10 minutes, until slightly reduced and thickened. Whisk in the butter, if using, until it is melted.

To serve, place Tomato Concassé on a plate and serve the veal on top, with the olives.

Note: Concassé simply means 'coarsely chopped'. The tomatoes can be pureed in a food processor or blender for a smoother sauce, if you like. Soaking in milk stops the eggplant from absorbing too much oil and becoming soggy—it is much healthier and tastier doing it this way. Instead of making individual servings, you could use one large piece of veal, as shown in the picture. In this case, cut into slices to serve.

mechoui

Serves 10–12

This is a traditional Moroccan countryside recipe, usually cooked on a barbecue or spit. It is done here in a conventional oven, but the flavours and aromas of outside cooking are something you should experience if possible.

marinade	
3 tablespoons olive oil	1 young milk-fed lamb (6–8kg/12–16lb)
3 garlic cloves, crushed	2 large brown onions, quartered
2 teaspoons grated ginger	250g (8oz) unsalted butter
3 teaspoons ground coriander	1 tablespoon salt
1 teaspoon ground cloves	2 teaspoons peppercorns
1 teaspoon ground black pepper	2 tablespoons cumin seeds
	1 teaspoon salt, extra

Preheat the oven to 250°C (475°F/Gas 9).

To make the marinade, place all the ingredients into a bowl and mix well.

Cut the lamb into quarters and rub the marinade all over (ask your butcher to cut the lamb for you when you purchase it). Place into a large oven dish with the onion quarters and bake for 30 minutes. Melt the butter together with the salt.

Reduce the heat to 150°C (300°F/Gas 2). Turn the lamb and rub with the salted butter. Cook for a further 30 minutes, or until the meat can be easily removed from the bone.

Meanwhile, toast the peppercorns and cumin seeds in a dry frying pan until fragrant. Remove from heat and grind coarsely in a mortar and pestle with the extra salt.

Transfer the meat to a serving platter, sprinkle with pepper and cumin seed mix and serve with your choice of Moroccan salad.

ostrich fillet with triple mash and caramelised parsnip

Serves 2

marinade

1 garlic clove, crushed

1 tablespoon chopped fresh rosemary

½ Preserved Lemon (see page 29), flesh only, chopped

2 tablespoons olive oil

pinch saffron threads

1 tablespoon chopped fresh thyme

2 x 200g (6½oz) ostrich fillets

3 tablespoons butter

3 tablespoons brown sugar

1 tablespoon lemon juice

6 small parsnips, scrubbed

sauce

½ cup (125ml/4fl oz) merlot wine

1 cup (250ml/8fl oz) chicken stock

½ cup (75g/2¼oz) pomegranate seeds

½ cup (60g/2oz) fresh raspberries

2 tablespoons Grenadine

1 tablespoon butter

oil, for frying

1 cup Garlic Potato Mash (see page 176)

1 cup Herbed Kumara (Sweet Potato) Mash (see page 177)

1 cup Green Pea and Artichoke Mash (see page 176)

Mix all the marinade ingredients together, add the ostrich fillets and rub all over to coat. Marinate in the refrigerator for 2 hours. Preheat the oven to 200°C (400°F/Gas 6).

Combine the butter, brown sugar and lemon juice in a small saucepan and heat gently, stirring to melt the butter and dissolve the sugar. Brush all over the parsnips, place into a shallow baking dish, uncovered, and roast for 30 minutes, brushing regularly with the butter and sugar mixture.

Take the ostrich fillet out of the marinade and set aside. Place the marinade into a saucepan over a high heat, sizzle then add the merlot and the stock. Bring to the boil and cook for 10 minutes, until reduced.

Lower the heat and add the pomegranate seeds and raspberries. Cook for 5 minutes then take off the heat and cool slightly. Process in a blender until smooth, then strain through a fine sieve into a clean saucepan. Place over medium heat, add the Grenadine and butter and simmer to reduce for a further 5 minutes. Cover and keep warm.

Heat a little oil in a frying pan and cook the ostrich fillets over high heat for 3–5 minutes each side for medium, depending on the thickness of the fillet.

To serve, place the ostrich fillets in the centre of serving plates. Spoon half the Garlic Potato Mash on top of each fillet, then half the Herbed Kumara (Sweet Potato) Mash and half the Green Pea and Artichoke Mash on top. Arrange the parsnip pieces around the stack, then pour the sauce around the base.

kidney kebabs
with harissa lentils

Serves 2

kebabs	harissa lentils
1 Preserved Lemon (see page 29), flesh only, chopped	1 cup (185g) green or brown lentils
2 tablespoons Harissa (see page 26)	3 cups (750ml/24fl oz) water
1 tablespoon chopped tarragon	salt and freshly ground black pepper, to taste
2 tablespoons olive oil	2 tablespoons olive oil
9 small lamb kidneys, halved lengthwise	2 green onions (scallions), finely chopped
9 bulb spring onions, halved lengthways	2 tablespoons Harissa (see page 26)
	400g (14oz) can crushed tomatoes

For the Kebabs, combine the Preserved Lemon, Harissa, tarragon and olive oil in a bowl. Add the kidneys and spring onions, coat well, cover and refrigerate for 30 minutes.

Thread the kidneys and spring onions, alternating each, onto six 25cm (10in) oiled skewers—threading the kidneys (cut side down) through the length, and the spring onions (cut side down) through the side.

Preheat a char grill or barbecue to hot and cook the kebabs for 5 minutes each side.

To prepare the Harissa Lentils, place the lentils into a saucepan and add the water. Bring to the boil and reduce the heat. Simmer, stirring occasionally, for about 25 minutes, until tender. Drain, season with salt and pepper, and set aside.

Heat the olive oil in a frying pan. Add the spring onions (scallions) and Harissa and cook for 1 minute. Add the tomatoes, reduce the heat and simmer for 5 minutes. Add the drained lentils, cook for a further 5 minutes to reduce and thicken. Take off the heat.

To serve, place Harissa Lentils in the centre of two plates and layer 3 kebabs on top of each.

GRILLED LAMB SOSATIES

Serves 2

500g (1lb) lamb backstrap (boneless loin)
1 tablespoon olive oil
1 brown onion, finely diced
1 garlic clove, crushed
2 bay leaves
1 tablespoon sweet Madras curry powder
½ teaspoon chilli powder
1 teaspoon salt

1 tablespoon brown sugar
juice of 1 lemon
1 cup (300g/10oz) apricot conserve (jelly)
½ cup (125ml/4fl oz) cream
1 large kumara (sweet potato), peeled
oil, for deep frying
6 tablespoons sour cream
2 tablespoons shredded Parmesan cheese

Cut the lamb into 6 strips about 12cm (4¾in) long and 2.5cm (1in) wide.

Heat the olive in a saucepan, and fry the onion and garlic until soft. Stir in the bay leaves, curry powder, chilli powder, salt and sugar. Cook for 5 minutes then add the lemon juice. Reduce the heat to low, add the apricot conserve (jelly) and cook for 10 minutes. Allow to cool, take out half and leave half in the pan.

Using half the sauce, marinate the lamb pieces for 10–15 minutes before threading lengthwise onto 6 oiled skewers.

Add the cream to the remaining sauce in the pan and simmer for 5 minutes.

Using a vegetable peeler, shred the kumara (sweet potato) thickly lengthwise. Deep fry in hot oil until crisp. Drain on absorbent paper.

Char grill the lamb skewers for about 3–5 minutes each side, until browned but still pink in the middle.

To serve, pour the creamy sauce onto plates and stack the crunchy kumara (sweet potato) shreds in the centre. Arrange the lamb in a pyramid shape. Garnish each plate with 3 dollops of sour cream placed between the lamb in the sauce, and sprinkle with Parmesan.

Afro Barbecue Chicken

Serves 2

2 chicken breast fillets

marinade

1 bunch flat leaf parsley, leaves picked
1 red onion, diced
4 garlic cloves
½ cup (125ml/4fl oz) olive oil
2 tablespoons red wine vinegar
1 tablespoon Harissa (see page 26)
1 teaspoon salt

sauce

400g (14oz) can crushed tomatoes
½ cup (125ml/4fl oz) coconut cream

8 small Red Pontiac potatoes, scrubbed
1 teaspoon hot paprika
1 teaspoon ground cumin
salt, to taste
2 tablespoons olive oil
lemon and lime slices, to garnish
flat leaf parsley, to garnish

Preheat the oven to 180°C (350°F/Gas 4). Slice the fillets horizontally into 3 large flat pieces.

To make the marinade, place the parsley, onion, garlic, olive oil, vinegar, Harissa and salt into a blender and process until smooth.

Coat the chicken pieces with half the marinade, and leave to sit while you prepare the sauce.

For the sauce, place the remaining marinade into a saucepan and add the tomatoes. Cook for 10 minutes on low heat, add the coconut cream and simmer for another 10 minutes.

Boil the potatoes (skin on) in salted water for 10-15 minutes until just cooked, cool slightly and cut into quarters. Season with combined paprika, cumin and salt. Toss with oil to coat, then roast for about 30 minutes, until browned and cooked through.

Barbecue or char grill the chicken for about 2 minutes each side, taking care not to overcook as the chicken will dry out.

To serve, place hot potato wedges in the centre of the plates. Pour the sauce around the wedges, and arrange the chicken pieces in a pyramid shape. Garnish with lemon and lime slices, and some fresh parsley leaves.

steamed chicken with vermicelli stuffing

Serves 4

2 x 1.2kg (2lb 7oz) chickens
1 teaspoon salt
1 teaspoon pepper
250g (8oz) bean thread vermicelli
(cellophane noodles)
250g (8oz) medium raw prawns (shrimp), peeled
100g (3½oz) large field mushrooms, sliced

1 tablespoon Harissa (see page 26)
½ bunch coriander (cilantro), chopped
1 cup (250ml/8fl oz) chicken stock
2 bay leaves
50g (1¾oz) butter, melted
1 teaspoon toasted cumin seeds, to garnish
steamed vegetables or salad, to serve

Wash and dry the chickens, trim off any fat. Rub all over with salt and pepper.

Break the vermicelli in half and plunge into boiling water for 1 minute to soften. Drain well.

Chop the prawn (shrimp) meat, combine with the mushrooms, vermicelli, Harissa, coriander (cilantro) and chicken stock. Stuff into the chicken cavities. Seal the openings with toothpicks or small skewers, or stitch if you like.

Put the chickens into a large steamer with water and bay leaves in the bottom (you may want to use chicken or vegetable stock). Steam the chickens for 1 hour 15 minutes, brushing regularly with butter.

To serve, sprinkle toasted cumin seeds over the chickens, and arrange on a large platter, with steamed vegetables or salad.

MROUZIA

Serves 4

1 tablespoon Ras el Hanout Spice Mix (see page 42)	250g (8oz) raisins
1 teaspoon saffron threads	4 onions, halved and thinly sliced
1 teaspoon Smen (see page 41)	1 tablespoon honey
1 cup (250ml/8fl oz) olive oil	2 tablespoons sugar
1 teaspoon salt	1 teaspoon ground cinnamon
8 baby lamb shanks (bone in)	100g (3½oz) roasted blanched almonds

Combine the Ras el Hanout, saffron, Smen, oil and salt. Use this mixture to marinate the lamb shanks for 30 minutes.

Heat a large saucepan and add the shanks with the marinade and brown all over for about 5 minutes. Cover the shanks with water and simmer over low heat, covered, for 30 minutes, until the shanks are tender.

Soak the raisins in cold water for 2 minutes then drain and dry.

Take the shanks out of the pot and set aside. Add the onion to the pan and cook for 5 minutes, then add the raisins and cook for 15 minutes on low heat. Add the honey and sugar and cook uncovered for 5 minutes to reduce the sauce. Return the lamb shanks to the pan and cook for a further 10 minutes. Add the cinnamon, stir through and take off the heat.

To serve, transfer the shanks to the centre of a large serving plate, cover with sauce and sprinkle almonds on top.

coriander chicken with crispy cumin potato jackets

Serves 4

4 grain-fed chicken breast fillets, with skin on
1 tablespoon cumin seeds, roasted and crushed
½ Preserved Lemon (see page 29), flesh only, chopped
2 tablespoons olive oil
1L (32fl oz) water
2 bunches coriander (cilantro), folded and tied

4 chicken necks
salt, to taste
2 tablespoons cream
1 tablespoon butter
2 tablespoons chopped coriander (cilantro)
Crispy Cumin Potato Jackets (see page 189), to serve

Make about 4 slits in the skin side of each chicken breast, about 1cm (⅜in) deep.

Fry the cumin seeds in a dry frying pan over medium heat until fragrant, crush in a mortar and pestle. Mix together half the crushed cumin seeds with the Preserved Lemon flesh and 1 tablespoon of the olive oil, rub this mixture into the chicken breasts and set aside to marinate.

Place the water into a saucepan, add the tied bunches of coriander (cilantro), the chicken necks and salt, bring to the boil. Cook until reduced to 2 cups (500ml/16fl oz).

Strain this coriander (cilantro) stock into a clean pan, add the remaining crushed cumin seeds, cream and half the butter. Simmer on low heat for about 10 minutes, until reduced, thickened and creamy. Sprinkle the chopped coriander (cilantro) over and remove from the heat.

In a hot frying pan, add the remaining olive oil and butter and cook the chicken, skin side down, for about 5 minutes, until golden brown. Turn over and cook another 10 minutes until just cooked and still juicy on the inside.

To serve, place Crispy Cumin Potato Jackets into the centre of each serving plate. Top with a chicken breast, and pour coriander sauce over the chicken and around the plate.

individual spatchcock (poussin) B'stilla

Serves 4

Spatchcock (poussin) is ideal for B'Stilla. Fried instead of baked, these B'Stilla are a variation on the more complicated large pastry, served mainly on special occasions.

2 free range spatchcocks (poussin) (300g/10oz) each)	¼ cup (40g/1½oz) blanched almonds
¼ cup Charmoula Marinade (see page 32)	3 teaspoons icing (confectioners') sugar
2 tablespoons olive oil	1 teaspoon ground cinnamon
pinch saffron threads, soaked in 1 cup (250ml/8fl oz) water	50g (1¾oz) butter
	1 tablespoon orange blossom water
4 eggs	16 20cm (8in) square filo pastry sheets
2 tablespoons chopped flat leaf parsley	2 tablespoons icing (confectioners') sugar
1 tablespoon olive oil, extra	2 tablespoons ground cinnamon

Cut the spatchcocks in half and marinate overnight in Charmoula Marinade.

Preheat the oven to 180°C (350°F/Gas 4). Heat the oil in a saucepan. Cook the spatchcock over high heat until browned on all sides. Add the saffron water and enough extra water to cover the spatchcock, bring to the boil. Reduce the heat and simmer for 20 minutes until cooked. Take out the spatchcock and set aside until cool enough to handle. Take the meat off the bones and chop. Set aside.

Reduce the stock in the saucepan until 1 cup (250ml/8fl oz) remains. Break the eggs into a bowl and whisk. Add the parsley and pour into the stock, whisking over a low heat until creamy. Set aside.

Heat the extra olive oil in a frying pan and cook the almonds for about 5 minutes, until golden. Sprinkle with the sugar and cinnamon, stir to coat evenly. Remove from the heat and allow to cool.

Melt the butter and add the orange blossom water. Brush the first pastry sheet with this mixture. Place a second sheet diagonally on top and brush, then a third and fourth sheet, brushing each. (The pastry sheets should be layered off-square from each other, so you see points of all the corners). Repeat this process until you have 4 stacks of 4 pastry sheets.

Divide the cooked spatchcock into 4 and place in the centre of each pastry stack. Spoon the creamy egg mixture on top of each and top this with the sweet almond mixture. Fold the pastry edges into the centre to cover the filling, forming a round shape. Brush the tops with butter mixture. Fry each B'stilla, top side down first, in a hot frying pan with a little olive oil for 5 minutes until golden. Turn and fry another 5 minutes. Place onto an oven tray and bake for 5 minutes.

To serve, dust the tops with icing (confectioners') sugar and cinnamon and serve hot.

seafood

Hassan's snapper with charmoula and tomato salsa

Serves 4

	Tomato Salsa
2kg (4lb) whole snapper, cleaned and scaled	4 ripe tomatoes, blanched and seeded
1 cup Charmoula Marinade (see page 32)	1 Lebanese cucumber, seeded
2 sticks celery, sliced	½ red onion
2 small ripe tomatoes, sliced	1 garlic clove, crushed
1 small red onion, peeled and sliced into rings	2 tablespoons chopped coriander (cilantro)
1 green capsicum (bell pepper), seeded and sliced into rings	1 tablespoon olive oil
1 Preserved Lemon (see page 29), quartered	2 teaspoons lemon juice
12 green olives	1 teaspoon ground cumin
	salt and freshly ground black pepper, to taste
	Harissa (see page 26), to serve

Score cuts into the thickest part of the fish. Rub Charmoula Marinade all over the fish, inside and out. Reserve leftover marinade. Marinate in the refrigerator for 1–2 hours.

Preheat oven to 230°C (450°F/Gas 8). Place sliced celery into the bottom of a baking dish (or tajine). Lay the fish on the celery, and arrange the tomatoes, onion, capsicum (bell pepper), Preserved Lemon and olives on top.

Pour the remaining Charmoula Marinade over the fish, cover tightly with foil and cook for 15 minutes. Reduce the heat to 150°C (300°F/Gas 2), remove foil and bake for a further 15 minutes, or until golden brown.

To make the Tomato Salsa, dice the tomato, cucumber and onion. Combine with the remaining ingredients.

Serve the fish with the Tomato Salsa and Harissa on the side.

spiced tuna with ooa salsa

Serves 4

2 tablespoons coriander seeds	750g (1½lb) long tuna fillet
2 tablespoons fennel seeds	salt and freshly ground black pepper
1 teaspoon cardamom seeds	olive oil, to fry
2 tablespoons cumin seeds	baby spinach leaves, to serve
1 teaspoon whole cloves	2 cups OOA Salsa (see page 167)

Preheat the oven to 180°C (350°F/Gas 4). Combine the coriander, fennel, cardamom and cumin seeds with cloves in a dry frying pan. Stir over a moderate heat for about 3 minutes, until fragrant. Transfer to a plate and allow to cool before finely grinding with a mortar and pestle.

Season the whole tuna fillet with salt and pepper and coat all over with the spice mix. Add a little olive oil to a hot frying pan and seal the tuna fillet on all sides for about 8 minutes. Transfer to an oven tray and cook in the oven for 5 minutes. Take out and slice the tuna into 4 slices (it should be rare on the inside).

Serve on a bed of spinach with OOA Salsa on the side.

saffron citrus chilli fish

Serves 4

1 lemon	1 tablespoon sugar
1 grapefruit	3 cups (750ml/24fl oz) fish stock
1 lime	2 tablespoons chopped coriander (cilantro)
4 oranges	½ cup (60g/2oz) plain (all purpose) flour
2 tablespoons extra virgin olive oil	salt and freshly ground black pepper to taste
1 small brown onion	4 deep sea perch or snapper fillets or
1 teaspoon saffron threads	orange roughy (approx 750g/1½ lb)
1 medium zucchini (courgette), diced	olive oil, for frying
2 tablespoons sweet chilli sauce	Saffron Risotto Cake (see page 170)

Finely grate the lemon, grapefruit, lime and orange rind; set aside. Peel the fruit, discarding all white pith and membrane, and dice the flesh.

Heat the olive oil in a large saucepan, add the onion, saffron and zucchini (courgette). Cook for 2 minutes, stir in the sweet chilli sauce and sugar and cook for 1 minute, until caramelised. Add the fish stock and bring to the boil.

Simmer for 10 minutes, then add the citrus fruits. Cook a further 10 minutes, until the sauce has reduced. Stir through the coriander, take off the heat and leave to stand.

Mix the grated rind, flour, salt and pepper together and use to lightly coat the fish.

Heat a little olive oil in a frying pan. Cook the fish fillets for about 3 minutes each side, depending on the thickness. Take care not to overcook.

Serve on top of Saffron Risotto Cake, with the citrus chilli sauce spooned over.

North African garlic prawns (shrimp)

Serves 4

2 tablespoons olive oil
½ cup minced garlic
1 Preserved Lemon (see page 29),
flesh only, chopped
juice of 1 lemon
3 tablespoons sweet paprika
1 tablespoon finely chopped red chilli

1 tablespoon salt
2 bunches flat leaf parsley, chopped
1 cup (250g/8oz) soft butter
20 raw king prawns (jumbo shrimp)
1 cup (250ml/8fl oz) coconut milk
mixed green leaf salad, to serve
Prepared Couscous (see page 175), to serve

Heat the olive oil in a saucepan. Fry the garlic for a few seconds then add the Preserved Lemon flesh, lemon juice, paprika, chilli, salt and parsley, cook for 5 minutes. Take off the heat and stir through the soft butter, allow to cool.

Prepare the prawns (shrimp) by peeling off the legs—leaving the shell, heads and tails intact. Split with a sharp knife on the underside where the legs were removed, without cutting all the way through. Stuff the parsley mixture into the prawns (shrimp), refrigerate for 30 minutes. Reserve leftover parsley mixture.

Barbecue or grill the prawns for about two minutes on each side—don't overcook.

Place remaining parsley mixture into a saucepan with the coconut milk and heat through, stirring (do not boil, as the butter will separate). Pour the sauce over the prawns and serve with mixed green leaf salad and Prepared Couscous.

GRILLED OCTOPUS, PRESERVED LEMON AND ROAST CAPSICUM SALAD WITH SAFFRON DRESSING

Serves 4

2 whole heads garlic
1 large red capsicum (bell pepper)
1 bunch bulb spring onions
1kg (2lb) baby octopus, cleaned and dried
2 tablespoons olive oil
1 Preserved Lemon (see page 29), sliced
mixed lettuce leaves
julienne vegetables, to garnish

SAFFRON DRESSING
2 egg yolks
½ teaspoon saffron threads
½ teaspoon Dijon mustard
½ Preserved Lemon (see page 29), flesh only
½ teaspoon white pepper
1 cup (250ml/8fl oz) extra virgin olive oil

Preheat the oven to 180°C (350°F/Gas 4). Roast the garlic, capsicum (bell pepper) and spring onions for about 20 minutes, until tender. Set the garlic aside for the dressing.

Pull the skin from the capsicum (bell pepper) and slice the flesh. Cut the spring onions in half lengthways.

Heat a char grill or barbecue. Toss the octopus with half the olive oil and Preserved Lemon in a bowl, coating the octopus thoroughly. Cook over high heat for a few minutes, until pink and tender. Toss the spring onion and capsicum (bell pepper) (keep a little aside for garnish) with the remaining olive oil and Preserved Lemon. Add the cooked octopus and mixed lettuce leaves. Arrange on a plate and drizzle with the Saffron Dressing. Serve garnished with julienne vegetables, and reserved red capsicum (bell pepper) strips.

To make the Saffron Dressing, squeeze the roasted garlic flesh into a food processor, add the remaining ingredients, apart from the oil. With the motor running, add the oil slowly, until the dressing becomes thick.

Grilled scallops on lemon grass and chive risotto

Serves 2

Risotto

5 cups (1.25L/40fl oz) fish stock
1 cup (250ml/8fl oz) dry white wine
2 sticks lemon grass, sliced into rings
2 tablespoons olive oil
2 cups (440g/15oz) arborio rice
3 tablespoons lemon juice
½ cup chopped chives
½ cup grated Parmesan cheese

10 scallops
90g (3oz) melted butter
freshly ground black pepper, to taste
2 tablespoons finely chopped coriander
   (cilantro), chopped
chopped chives and slivered lemon rind, to garnish

Place the stock, wine and lemon grass into a saucepan and bring to the boil over medium heat. Strain to remove the lemon grass. Heat the olive oil in a large saucepan, and fry the rice for 1 minute.

Add the stock a bit at a time to the rice, stirring as you go. Cook, stirring and adding stock, for about 20 minutes, until the rice is tender. Stir through the lemon juice, chives and Parmesan. Cover and keep warm.

Mix the scallops with butter, pepper and coriander (cilantro). Char grill, barbecue or pan fry for a couple of minutes each side until opaque, taking care not to overcook.

Place the risotto onto plates and pile scallops on top. Garnish with chives and slivers of lemon rind and serve immediately.

Garlic spiced tuna with couscous salad

Serves 4

	couscous salad
2 red chillies, finely chopped	2 tablespoons olive oil
3 tablespoons olive oil	1 cup (160g/5½oz) pickled cocktail onions, halved
3 tablespoons Worcestershire sauce	2 tomatoes, peeled, seeded and diced
2 tablespoons chopped coriander (cilantro)	4 spring onions (scallions), sliced diagonally
½ Preserved Lemon (see page 29), finely chopped	3 cups Prepared Couscous (see page 175)
3 garlic cloves, sliced	1 teaspoon ground black pepper
1 teaspoon sea salt	1 Lebanese cucumber, seeded and diced
4 tuna steaks	2 tablespoons lemon juice
	2 Roma tomatoes, halved and char grilled, to serve

Combine the chillies, olive oil, Worcestershire sauce, coriander (cilantro), Preserved Lemon, garlic and sea salt in a bowl. Add the tuna steaks and marinate for 2 hours in the refrigerator. Take out 30 minutes before cooking.

To make the Couscous Salad, heat the oil in a large frying pan, add the pickled onions, tomatoes and spring onions (scallions) and cook for 3 minutes. Add the Prepared Couscous and mix thoroughly; remove from the heat. Add the pepper, cucumber and lemon juice, mix through.

Heat a char grill or frying pan until very hot, cook the marinated tuna for 1 minute on each side (tuna is best served rare). Serve topped with garlic slices and a tomato half, on a bed of Couscous Salad.

Barbecued Salmon and Prawns in Banana Leaves

Serves 3

18 raw king prawns (jumbo shrimp)
¼ cup Harissa (see page 26)
2 tablespoons honey
1 tablespoon chopped coriander (cilantro)
1 tablespoon Preserved Lemon (see page 29), flesh only, finely chopped

200g (7oz) fresh salmon steak
18 mint leaves
banana leaves, cut into 18 thin strips (the width of the prawns)
peanut oil, to cook

Peel the prawns (shrimp), leaving the heads and tails intact. Split with a sharp knife on the underside where the legs were removed, without cutting all the way through.

Combine the Harissa, honey, coriander (cilantro) and Preserved Lemon. Add the prawns and marinate for 15 minutes.

Cut the salmon into 18 strips, place one into each of the prawns and cover with a mint leaf. Wrap each of the prawns in a banana leaf and thread lengthways onto short bamboo skewers. Lightly brush a barbecue hot plate with peanut oil and cook the prawns over a high heat, brushing regularly with marinade, for about 3 minutes on each side.

Put the remaining marinade into a saucepan and bring to the boil; cool slightly. Pour over the prawns before serving.

mixed charmoula
seafood grill

Serves 2

1 cup Charmoula Marinade (see page 32)
6 small sardines, gutted
2 lemons, sliced into 3 pieces
2 limes, sliced into 3 pieces

6 raw king prawns (jumbo shrimp), legs removed
6 perch fillets or orange roughy (the same thickness as the sardines)
1 bunch coriander (cilantro), stalks removed
1 bunch flat leaf parsley, stalks removed

Put the Charmoula Marinade into a food processor and process until smooth. Rub the seafood pieces all over, inside and out, with the Marinade.

Arrange the seafood on a hinged wire rack with a row of sardines, then alternating citrus slices, then a row of prawns, another row of alternating citrus, then the perch fillets.

Close the wire rack and place over medium to hot coals and grill until skin of the sardines is crispy—about 5 minutes each side.

To serve, line the bottom of a large platter with the coriander and parsley. Arrange the grilled seafood and citrus on the top.

whole fish stuffed with vermicelli seafood

Serves 6

1.5kg (3lb) whole fish (mackerel or trout)
juice of 1 lemon
3 cloves garlic, crushed
2 tablespoons sweet paprika
1 tablespoon hot paprika
1 tablespoon salt
1 teaspoon black pepper
1 bunch flat leaf parsley, chopped
1 bunch coriander (cilantro), chopped
1 cup (250ml/8fl oz) olive oil

stuffing

100g (3½oz) bean thread vermicelli
  (cellophane noodles)
250g (½lb) raw prawns (shrimp)
250g (½lb) calamari (squid) tubes, cleaned
  and diced
200g (6½oz) button mushrooms, thinly sliced
100g (3½oz) green olives, pitted
roasted tomatoes and fresh lemon wedges, to serve

Scale, gut and wash the fish (you may like to have your fishmonger do this for you).

Place the lemon juice, garlic, sweet and hot paprika, salt and pepper, parsley, coriander and olive oil into a large bowl. Mix well and use half this mixture (reserve other half) to rub all over the fish inside and out. Put the fish aside to marinate in the refrigerator for 30 minutes.

Preheat the oven to 180°C (350°F/Gas 4).

To make the Stuffing, plunge the vermicelli noodles into boiling water for 1 minute to soften. Drain well. Peel and devein the prawns (shrimp); roughly chop.

Heat a frying pan over high heat. Add the reserved marinade and the calamari and fry for 2 minutes. Turn off the heat and add the prawns, mushrooms, green olives and vermicelli, mix well together. Place this stuffing inside the fish. Put the stuffed fish into a shallow baking dish, cover with foil and bake for 30 minutes. Serve hot, with roasted tomatoes and fresh lemon wedges.

seafood couscous

Serves 4

stock

500g heads and bones of fish
(ask your fishmonger)
2 red onions, peeled and quartered
250g (8oz) tomatoes, halved and seeded
½ teaspoon saffron threads
1 sprig thyme
½ Preserved Lemon (see page 29), skin only
10 whole black peppercorns
4 tablespoons olive oil
4 sprigs coriander (cilantro)
4 sprigs flat leaf parsley
4 garlic cloves, peeled
¼ teaspoon hot paprika
salt, to taste

8 baby carrots
4 baby turnips
8 bulb spring onions
4 yellow baby squash
4 green baby squash
500g (1lb) couscous

fish balls

2 tablespoons Harissa (see page 26)
1 tablespoon chopped thyme
1 tablespoon chopped coriander
1 garlic clove, crushed
1 cup small peeled prawns (baby shrimp)
500g (1lb) boneless perch fillet or orange roughy
500g (1lb) boneless sardine fillets

sauce

1 tablespoon Harissa (see page 26)
400g (14oz) can crushed tomatoes
1 tablespoon chopped coriander (cilantro)

16 raw king prawns (jumbo shrimp)
4 x 200g firm fish cutlets (such as swordfish or tuna)
Harissa (see page 26), to serve

In the bottom of a couscoussier or steamer, combine all the stock ingredients and cover with 1.2L (38fl oz) water and slowly bring to the boil. Skim off any froth or impurities, reduce the heat, cover and simmer for 15 minutes. Add the vegetables and cook in the stock while steaming the couscous.

Prepare the couscous and steam over the stock, following the instructions given on page 175.

While the vegetables and couscous are cooking, prepare the fish balls. Mix together the Harissa, thyme, coriander and garlic and combine with the prawns (shrimp), perch and sardines. Put through a mincer, or finely chop and mix together (a food processor would make the mixture too pasty). Form into balls about the size of a golf ball. Set aside.

To make the sauce, place 3 cups (750ml/24fl oz) of the stock (out of the couscoussier) into a saucepan with the Harissa, tomatoes and coriander. Bring to the boil and cook for 10 minutes. Put the king prawns (jumbo shrimp), fish cutlets and fish balls into the sauce and poach for 5 minutes. Take off the heat and stand, covered, for 5 minutes.

To serve, arrange the couscous in a ring around the edge of a large shallow serving bowl. Place the vegetables on top of the couscous. Put the fish cutlets in the centre and top with the prawns. Arrange the fish balls around the outside of the couscous. Drizzle with the sauce just before serving, or serve the sauce on the side in a bowl with a small dish of Harissa.

seafood pasta

Serves 3–4

This versatile recipe can also be made with chicken, vegetables or any combination you desire. The sauce is the secret, and it is extremely low in fat.

2 cups (180g/2oz) penne pasta	1 tablespoon tomato paste (tomato concentrate)
cooking spray	salt and freshly ground black pepper, to taste
1–2 garlic cloves, crushed	300g (10oz) raw prawns (shrimp), peeled
1 brown onion, finely chopped	10 scallops
400g can (14oz) evaporated skim (non-fat) milk	chopped fresh herbs
400g can (14oz) crushed tomatoes	

Cook the penne in a large pan of boiling water until al dente.

Lightly spray a frying pan with cooking spray. Fry the garlic and onion until tender. Add the milk, tomatoes, and tomato paste; season with salt and pepper. Simmer the sauce for 3 minutes.

Add the seafood and herbs. Cover the pan and simmer for a further 3 minutes (or until the seafood becomes opaque). Add the cooked pasta and mix through, or serve the sauce over the pasta if you like.

Note: Use your choice of one or a combination of fresh herbs, such as dill, flat leaf parsley or basil.

Garlic Baked Blue-Eye Cod with Tamarillo Dressing

Serves 4

4 tamarillos, halved	**Dressing**
1 tablespoon olive oil	2 tamarillos, peeled
4 blue-eye cod fillets or turbot or halibut	1 tablespoon chopped lemon thyme leaves
4 garlic cloves, sliced	½ cup (125ml/4fl oz) olive oil
1 tablespoon chopped lemon thyme leaves	juice of 1 lime
salt and freshly ground black pepper, to taste	salt and freshly ground black pepper, to taste
500g (1lb) baby spinach leaves	
1 Preserved Lemon (see page 29), cut into wedges	

Preheat the oven to 180°C (350°F/Gas 4). Place the tamarillos, cut side up, on a baking tray lined with non-stick baking paper and brush with olive oil. Bake for 20 minutes, until soft and lightly browned.

Meanwhile, place the cod fillets on a baking tray lined with non-stick baking paper and sprinkle with garlic slices, lemon thyme, salt and pepper. Place in the oven with the tamarillos and bake for 10–15 minutes, until cooked.

To make the dressing, blend all the ingredients together in a food processor until smooth.

Serve cod on a bed of spinach leaves, with roasted tamarillos and wedges of preserved lemon or lime, drizzled with the dressing.

vegetables, salads
and accompaniments

zufu zaafook

Serves 4

4 eggplants (aubergines)
½ cup (125ml/4fl oz) olive oil
3 ripe tomatoes
2 garlic cloves, crushed
2 teaspoons sweet paprika
1 teaspoon ground cumin

salt and freshly ground black pepper, to taste
½ cup (125ml/4fl oz) white vinegar
½ bunch coriander (cilantro), chopped
1 Preserved Lemon (see page 29), sliced
12 green olives
bread, to serve

Preheat the oven to 200°C (400°F/Gas 6). Cut the eggplants (aubergines) in half, then score deeply into large cubes (do not slice through the skin). Brush the cut surfaces with half the olive oil. Place on an oven tray and bake for 10–15 minutes or until cooked. Remove from the oven and cut into large cubes.

Make a small cut in the skin of the tomatoes, plunge into boiling water. Drain, then when cool enough to handle remove the skin and seeds. Dice the flesh.

Heat the remaining olive oil in a frying pan, fry the garlic briefly then add the tomatoes, paprika, cumin, salt and pepper and eggplant (aubergine). Bring to the boil, stirring occasionally. Add the vinegar, coriander, half the sliced Preserved Lemon and simmer for 10 minutes.

Let stand for a few minutes (should be served warm—not hot), garnish with the olives and remaining sliced Preserved Lemon.

Serve with bread.

sweet chickpeas (garbanzos)

Makes about 6 cups

Chickpeas (garbanzos) of this style are often used in dishes to garnish and add flavour.

500g (1lb) dried chickpeas (garbanzos)	½ teaspoon saffron threads
enough water to cover chickpeas	1 tablespoon ground cinnamon
1L (32fl oz) water	½ cup (125ml/4fl oz) honey
salt, to taste	juice of 2 oranges
1 brown onion, halved and finely sliced	2 tablespoons orange blossom water
2 bay leaves	200g (6½oz) sultanas (golden raisins)

Cover the chickpeas with water and soak overnight. Drain and transfer to a saucepan. Add the water, boil for about 30 minutes, until the water has reduced and is just covering the peas.

Add the salt, onion, bay leaves, saffron threads, cinnamon, honey, orange juice and orange blossom water and cook for a further 10 minutes.

Stir in the sultanas (golden raisins), to just soften. Drain and store in refrigerator. These can be kept for up to a week, heat prior to serving.

fresh artichoke, fennel and broad bean (fava bean) stew

Serves 4

4 tablespoons extra virgin olive oil
1 bulb spring onion, halved
2 garlic cloves, finely chopped
2 tablespoons chopped flat leaf parsley
4 large artichokes (or 6 medium), trimmed and thinly sliced
1 large fennel bulb, halved lengthwise, core removed, sliced thickly across

500g (1lb) broad beans (fava beans), shelled but not peeled
150g (5oz) snow peas (mange-tout)
125g (4oz) shredded greens (see Note)
salt and freshly ground black pepper, to taste
grated Parmesan cheese, to serve
extra virgin olive oil and crusty bread, to serve

Combine the oil and onion in a large saucecpan and cook over a moderate heat for about 8 minutes, until soft. Add the garlic and parsley and cook for a further minute. Stir in the artichokes and cook for a few minutes, then repeat with the fennel.

Stir in the broad beans (fava beans) and snow peas (mange-tout). Add the greens and stir until beginning to wilt. Add enough water to cover the vegetables and season with salt and pepper. Bring to the boil then simmer with the lid ajar for 20–30 minutes, until the vegetables are tender, stirring occasionally.

Adjust the seasoning and serve in heated bowls with a separate dish of grated Parmesan and some extra olive oil to drizzle onto the stew. Serve with plenty of crusty bread.

Note: Use greens such as chicory, curly endive, English spinach or watercress.

smashed green olive and ruby grapefruit salad

Serves 4

250g (8oz) green olives
2 ruby grapefruit, peeled and segmented
¼ cup (10g/⅓oz) flat leaf parsley
100g (3½oz) snowpea sprouts (watercress)
½ cup (75g/2¼oz) roasted hazelnuts

1 avocado, chopped
½ cup (75g/2¼oz) pomegranate seeds
2 tablespoons olive oil
juice of ½ lemon
freshly ground black pepper

Place the olives between layers of absorbent paper and hit each olive with a mallet or rolling pin to release the stones.

Place the olives, grapefruit, parsley, snowpea (mange-tout) sprouts, hazelnuts and avocado onto a serving plate. Mix pomegranate seeds, oil, lemon juice and pepper and pour over salad. Allow to stand for 10–15 minutes prior to serving, for the flavours to mix and enhance.

couscous, Asparagus and chickpea (Garbanzo) salad with creamy walnut Dressing

Serves 4

2 bunches asparagus spears
75g (2¼oz) snow peas (mange-tout), topped
1 small butter lettuce, washed and leaves separated
1 small mignonette or coral lettuce (curly endive), washed and leaves separated
2 cups Prepared Couscous (see page 175), cooled
300g (10oz) Moroccan Chickpeas (garbanzos) (see page 166)
sweet paprika, to dust

walnut Dressing

30g (1oz) walnuts
½ cup (125g/4oz) fat reduced natural yoghurt
2 tablespoons lemon juice
1 teaspoon finely grated lemon rind
1 tablespoon thyme leaves
salt and freshly ground pepper, to taste

Steam the asparagus for 2 minutes or until tender yet still crisp. Place the snow peas (mange-tout) into a heatproof bowl and cover with boiling water, stand for 1 minute. Plunge asparagus and snow peas (mange-tout) immediately into cold water, then drain well.

Arrange lettuce leaves on a serving plate and place couscous in the centre, top with snow peas (mange-tout), Moroccan Chickpeas (garbanzos) and asparagus.

To make the dressing, place the walnuts, yoghurt, lemon juice, rind, thyme, salt and pepper in a food processor or blender and process until well combined. Drizzle over the salad.

Dust lightly with sweet paprika to serve.

moroccan chickpeas (garbanzos)

Makes about 3 cups

300g (10oz) dried chickpeas (garbanzos)	4 garlic cloves, crushed
1L (32fl oz) water	1 tablespoon ground cumin
1 tablespoon salt	1 tablespoon olive oil

Cover the chickpeas (garbanzos) with water and soak overnight. Drain and transfer to a saucepan. Add the water, boil for 30 minutes, until soft. Drain and cool.

Mix together the salt, garlic, cumin and olive oil and stir through cooled chickpeas (garbanzos). These can be used on salads, or as a garnish for various meat, chicken and fish dishes.

confit of cabbage

Serves 4

½ red cabbage, sliced	150ml (5fl oz) orange juice
1 red onion, finely sliced	100ml (3½fl oz) red wine vinegar
2 Granny Smith apples, diced	1 cup (200g/7oz) brown sugar
3 whole cloves	100g (3½oz) gelatine powder
1 tablespoon ground cinnamon	125g (4oz) redcurrants

Mix all ingredients together and marinate in the refrigerator overnight.

Cook the mixture in a large, heavy-based saucepan on low heat for 1 hour, covered.

Take off the lid and cook for a further 30 minutes, on low heat, allowing the mixture to reduce and caramelise. Stir occasionally. This will keep refrigerated for weeks.

Note: Great to serve with game meats. Layer confit onto a plate, spoon mashed potato on top, then the sliced rare meat.

ooa salsa

Serves 4

2 red capsicums (bell peppers)	10 mint leaves
4 Roma tomatoes	½ bunch coriander (cilantro)
200g piece butternut pumpkin (butternut squash)	2 cloves garlic
1 tablespoon honey	4 tablespoons olive oil
2 ruby grapefruit	1 tablespoon red wine vinegar
10 basil leaves	salt and freshly ground black pepper, to taste

Preheat the oven to 180°C (350°F/Gas 4). Cut the capsicums (bell peppers) into large flat pieces, discarding the seeds and membrane. Grill (broil) skin side up, until the skin is black. Peel and cut into 1cm (⅜in) squares.

Make a small slit in the skin of the tomatoes, and plunge into boiling water. Dip into cold water then peel away the skin. Cut in half lengthways, seed and cut into 1cm (⅜in) dices.

Cut the pumpkin (squash) into 1cm (⅜in) cubes. Coat in honey and put into a shallow roasting dish. Roast for 10–15 minutes until golden, take out and cool.

Peel the grapefruit, making sure to remove all the white pith as well. Cut into 1cm (⅜in) cubes.

Combine the capsicum, tomatoes, pumpkin and grapefruit in a glass bowl and gently mix together. Chop the herbs and add just before serving. Whisk the oil and vinegar with salt and pepper, and drizzle over the salsa.

stuffed capsicum with herb couscous and walnut yoghurt dressing

Serves 4 as a starter

½ cup (90g/3oz) Prepared Couscous
2 tablespoons olive oil
2 medium red capsicums (bell peppers), halved and seeded
2 medium green capsicums (bell peppers) halved and seeded
200g (7oz) mushrooms, quartered
4 spring onions (scallions), chopped
2 tablespoons chopped mint
2 tablespoons chopped coriander (cilantro)
salt and freshly ground black pepper, to taste
2 large Roma tomatoes, blanched, peeled and cut lengthways into quarters
basil leaves and mixed olives, to garnish

walnut dressing

30g (1oz) walnuts
½ cup (125g/4oz) fat reduced natural yoghurt
2 tablespoons lemon juice
1 teaspoon finely grated lemon rind
1 tablespoon thyme leaves

Preheat the oven to 180°C (350°F/Gas 4). Prepare the couscous according to the instructions on page 175.

Heat half the olive oil in a large frying pan, add the capsicums (bell peppers) and cook over medium heat for about 8 minutes turning once, or until softened slightly.

Remove from the pan and place in an oiled ovenproof dish cut side up.

Heat the remaining olive oil in the frying pan and cook the mushrooms over high heat for 3–4 minutes or until they start to colour. Reduce the heat to low and add the onions, couscous, mint and coriander (cilantro). Cook for 2–3 minutes. Season generously with salt and pepper.

Spoon the filling into the capsicum (bell pepper) halves, place 1 tomato quarter on top of each. Cover the dish with foil and bake for 30 minutes or until capsicum is tender.

To make the dressing, place the walnuts, yoghurt, lemon juice, rind and thyme in a food processor or blender and process until well combined. Drizzle over the capsicums (bell peppers) to serve. Garnish plates with basil leaves and mixed olives.

saffron Risotto cake

Serves 12

100ml (3½fl oz) olive oil
1 large brown onion, grated
8 garlic cloves, crushed
2 tomatoes, peeled, seeded and diced
1L (32fl oz) chicken stock
400g (13oz) arborio rice
100ml (3½fl oz) orange blossom water

1 teaspoon saffron threads, soaked in
2 tablespoons water
6 fresh lime leaves, torn and chopped
1 cup (90g/3oz) chopped mushrooms
1 teaspoon freshly ground black pepper
80g (2½oz) butter
100g (3½oz) grated Parmesan cheese
vegetable oil, for frying

Heat the oil in a large saucepan and fry the onion and garlic, stir in the diced tomatoes and cook until soft and sizzling. Add half the stock and bring to the boil.

Rinse the rice and add to the boiling stock, stirring constantly until the rice is well coated. Add the orange blossom water and the saffron, and cook for about 15 minutes, stirring constantly.

When the rice starts to get a little sticky, add the rest of the stock, lime leaves and mushrooms and cook for a further 5 minutes. The rice should become creamy.

Add the black pepper, stir in the butter and Parmesan cheese and mix well. Pour into a tray (about 4.5cm/1½in deep), and refrigerate until set.

Preheat the oven to 200°C (400°F/Gas 6). Cut the risotto cake into squares. Heat a little oil in a frying pan, seal the risotto cake on both sides. Heat through in the oven for 5 minutes.

stuffed artichokes on beetroot (beet) puree

Serves 4

stuffing	beetroot (beet) puree
1 garlic clove, crushed	3 fresh beetroot (beets), unpeeled, with 6cm (2in) of stem left on
1 small red onion, finely diced	2 tablespoons olive oil
1 small carrot, finely chopped	1 teaspoon finely grated orange rind
200g (7oz) button mushrooms, sliced	½ cup (125ml/4fl oz) orange juice
1 teaspoon olive oil	salt and black pepper, to taste
2 sprigs tarragon, chopped	
salt, to taste	
1 teaspoon freshly ground black pepper	8 fresh artichokes
200g (7oz) unsalted pistachio kernels, roasted and crushed	juice of 1 lemon
	1 teaspoon sugar

To make the stuffing, fry the garlic, onion, carrot and mushrooms in the olive oil for about 10 minutes, until just tender. Add the tarragon, salt and pepper, and pistachios, mix through and set aside.

For the Beetroot (beet) Puree, preheat the oven to 200°C (400°F/Gas 6). Brush the beetroot with half the olive oil and roast for 45 minutes. Leave the oven on. Allow to cool then peel. Place into a food processor with the orange rind, orange juice, remaining olive oil, salt and pepper and process until smooth.

To prepare the artichokes, peel off the tough outer leaves and cut in half lengthways. Take out the hairy part from the middle. Cook the artichokes in boiling water for 5 minutes, then rinse under cold water and dry.

Mix the lemon juice with the sugar, coat the artichokes with this mixture, then top with the mushroom mixture. Place on a baking tray and brush with olive oil. Bake for 15 minutes.

To serve, pour Beetroot (Beet) Puree into a circle on 4 plates and top each with 2 artichoke halves.

eggplant stack

Serves 2

2 medium eggplants (aubergines)	1 teaspoon ground cumin
2 tablespoons salt	150g (5oz) log goat cheese
1 cup (250ml/8fl oz) milk	8 sun-dried tomatoes
plain (all purpose) flour, to coat	10 green olives, crushed
1 cup (250ml/8fl oz) olive oil	½ bunch basil, leaves picked
1 red capsicum (bell pepper)	1 Preserved Lemon (see page 29)
salt and freshly ground black pepper, to taste	sprigs of dill and coriander leaves, to garnish

Cut the eggplant (aubergine) lengthways into 1cm (½in) thick slices. Take 6 of the largest slices, sprinkle with the salt and stand for 30 minutes to draw out any bitterness. Rinse and pat dry.

Soak the eggplant slices in milk for 2 minutes, then coat lightly with flour to seal. Pan-fry in half the olive oil for about 3 minutes each side, until golden brown.

Cut the capsicum (bell pepper) into large flat pieces, discarding the seeds and membrane. Cook skin side up under a hot grill (broiler), until the skin blackens. Allow to cool, then peel off the skin and cut the flesh into strips.

Mix the salt, pepper and cumin together and sprinkle over eggplant (aubergine) and capsicum (bell pepper). Cut a slice from the goat cheese log, and crumble the rest.

On 2 large serving plates, place a slice of eggplant (aubergine) in centre, top with capsicum (bell pepper) strips (reserve a few for garnishing), then crumbled goat cheese. Add another eggplant (aubergine) layer, sun-dried tomatoes, crushed olives, goat cheese, and about 5 basil leaves. Top with a final eggplant (aubergine) layer.

Fry the slice of cheese briefly to lightly brown, and cut in half. Place on top of the stack.

Place the remaining olive oil into a blender with the flesh of the Preserved Lemon and blend until smooth, drizzle onto each eggplant stack and around the plate.

Cut the Preserved Lemon skin into thin strips, use to decorate around the plate with the remaining capsicum (bell pepper) strips and basil leaves. Sprinkle with freshly ground black pepper and a little more cumin if you wish, and top with sprigs of dill and coriander leaves.

Note: Soaking in milk stops the eggplant from absorbing too much oil and becoming soggy—it is much healthier and tastier doing it this way.

prepared couscous

Serves 4

For the best couscous, it is a good idea to invest in a couscoussier. This is a large aluminium, brass or stainless steel pot which holds a tight fitting, fine holed colander on top, and a lid.

For sweet dishes

4L (128fl oz) water	2 cinnamon sticks
1 tablespoon salt	pinch saffron threads
3 bay leaves	500g (1lb) couscous
½ teaspoon black peppercorns	100g (3½oz) butter

Pour 3L (96fl oz) of the water into the bottom of the couscoussier, add half the salt, bay leaves, peppercorns and cinnamon sticks and bring to the boil.

In a saucepan combine the remaining water with the saffron and remaining salt, and heat almost to boiling point.

Put the couscous into a shallow bowl and cover with half the saffron water, allow to soak up the liquid for 10 minutes. Using a wooden spoon gently stir the couscous, then using your fingers, separate the grains and rub out all lumps (doing this at the beginning prevents couscous becoming lumpy).

Place cheesecloth around the lip of the bottom part of the couscoussier, and put the top part in place (the cloth prevents any steam escaping - allowing it to steam through the couscous).

Spread the couscous evenly into the top part. Wait until the steam starts to come through the grain (making sure there is no steam escaping out between the two pots), and steam (uncovered) for 5 minutes. Take out the couscous, return to the shallow bowl, add 1 cup (250ml/8fl oz) of the remaining saffron water, stir through and remove lumps as before. Leave to stand for 10 minutes before placing back into the couscoussier and steaming, as before, for another 5 minutes.

Take out the couscous and return to the bowl once more, add the remaining saffron water, fluff up the grains and remove any lumps with your fingers. Add the butter and mix through with your fingers (butter or oil is always added after the last steaming to seal the grain).

Couscous can be kept refrigerated for up to 1 week, and can be used hot or cold.

For savoury dishes

Follow the same steaming process as for sweet dishes, but use a vegetable, fish or meat stock in the base of the couscoussier. These can be flavoured with bay leaves, peppercorns, onion and garlic. There are numerous combinations of flavours and not a lot of limitations—experiment with your favourites for stock. Instead of using butter to seal the grain, you could use extra virgin olive oil or Smen (see page 41).

garlic potato mash

Serves 6

1kg (2lb) medium potatoes
5 garlic cloves
50g (1¾oz) butter

salt and freshly ground black pepper, to taste
300ml (10fl oz) cream

Preheat the oven to 200°C (400°F/Gas 6). Scrub the potatoes and boil whole, with skin on, in salted water for 30 minutes. Drain, peel and mash with potato masher.

Meanwhile, roast the whole garlic cloves for about 10–15 minutes, until soft. Cool slightly, then peel off the skin.

Combine the garlic, butter, salt and pepper in a saucepan. Mash together over low heat, stir in the cream. Gradually add the mashed potato, stirring constantly, until all blended. Add more salt and pepper to taste if required.

green pea and artichoke mash

Serves 6

100g (3½oz) butter
1 tablespoon olive oil
½ brown onion, diced
4 garlic cloves, crushed

500g (1lb) frozen green peas, thawed
500g (1lb) canned artichoke hearts, drained
1 cup (250ml/8fl oz) coconut cream
salt and white pepper, to taste

Heat the butter and olive oil in a saucepan. Add the onion and garlic and fry until soft.

Add the peas and artichoke hearts, and cook over high heat, stirring, for 10 minutes.

Add the coconut cream and simmer for 20 minutes. Take off the heat, season with salt and pepper. Cool slightly then process in a food processor until smooth.

Herbed kumara (sweet potato) mash

Serves 6

1kg (2lb) kumara (sweet potatoes)
1 tablespoon olive oil
50g (1¾oz) butter
2 garlic cloves, crushed
1 teaspoon chopped oregano
1 tablespoon chopped thyme

1 tablespoon chopped coriander (cilantro)
1 tablespoon chopped tarragon
300ml (10fl oz) milk
salt, to taste
1 teaspoon cracked black pepper

Peel the kumara (sweet potatoes) and cut into cubes. Cook in boiling salted water for 20 minutes or until tender, drain and set aside.

Heat the olive oil and butter in a large saucepan. Fry the garlic briefly, add the oregano, thyme, coriander and tarragon. Cook for about 4 minutes, until fragrant.

Add the kumara (sweet potatoes) and mix through. Add the milk and simmer for about 10 minutes. Season with salt and pepper, take off the heat and mash until smooth.

moroccan glazed
carrot salad

Serves 2

A delicious combination of sweet and sour flavours, this salad is best served chilled.
Great with other salads, or as an appetizer or side dish.

2 large carrots	¼ teaspoon chilli powder
3 tablespoons olive oil	½ teaspoon salt
2 teaspoons white vinegar	2 tablespoons chopped flat leaf parsley
3 teaspoons icing (confectioners') sugar	1 cos (romaine) lettuce heart
1 teaspoon sweet paprika	

Peel the carrots and cut in half lengthways. Using a small sharp knife or an apple corer, remove the core and discard. Slice the rest diagonally into 1cm (⅜in) pieces. Cook in boiling salted water for about 10 minutes until just soft. Plunge into cold water to cool and stop cooking, drain and dry.

Combine the oil, vinegar, sugar, paprika, chilli powder, salt and parsley in a glass bowl, and whisk until it is the consistency of honey. Add the carrots and stir to glaze.

Break up the lettuce onto a serving platter and spoon glazed carrot into the centre.

moroccan summer salad

Serves 4

200g (6½oz) mixed leaves (see Note)
1 bunch flat leaf parsley, leaves picked
1 bunch coriander (cilantro), leaves picked
1 bunch mint, leaves picked
½ bunch basil, leaves picked
1 orange, peeled and segmented
1 grapefruit, peeled and segmented
½ cup Moroccan Dried Black Olives, pitted
(see page 39)
½ cup (60g/2oz) shredded fresh coconut

dressing

½ cup (125ml/4fl oz) coconut cream
1 tablespoon orange blossom water
1 tablespoon Malibu liqueur
½ Preserved Lemon (see page 29) flesh only, chopped
½ cup (125ml/4fl oz) orange juice

Wash and dry the mixed leaves. Place into a glass bowl with the parsley, coriander (cilantro), mint, basil, orange, grapefruit, and Moroccan Dried Black Olives. Toss together.

To make the dressing, place all the ingredients into a small bowl and whisk well.

Just before serving, sprinkle the salad with shredded coconut and drizzle with dressing.

Note: Use leaves such as different types of lettuce, spinach, rocket (arugula) or watercress.

char Grilled vegetables with Yoghurt Dip

Serves 4

	marinade
1 medium eggplant (aubergine)	2 tablespoons olive oil
1 medium kumara (sweet potato), peeled	1 tablespoon Harissa (see page 26)
1 green capsicum (bell pepper), halved and seeded	2 tablespoons chopped coriander (cilantro)
1 red capsicum (bell pepper), halved and seeded	juice of ½ lemon
3 medium zucchinis (courgettes)	½ cup Yoghurt Dip (see page 39)
1 bunch asparagus	
16 snow peas (mange-tout)	
2 leeks	

Wash and dry all the vegetables. Cut the eggplant (aubergine), kumara (sweet potatoes), capsicums (bell peppers) and zucchinis (courgettes) into 1cm (⅜in) thick lengths.

Cut the woody ends from the asparagus and top the snow peas (mange-tout). Trim the leeks and cut into 2 or 3 pieces (depending on length), then cut in half lengthways. Push a toothpick through the pieces of leek to hold them together while cooking.

Whisk all the marinade ingredients together. Toss the vegetables in the marinade, coating thoroughly.

Cook the vegetables on a hot barbecue or char grill for 5 minutes each side. Serve hot, on a platter with a bowl of Yoghurt Dip in the middle

spinach salad with preserved lemon

Serves 4

1 kg (2lb) baby spinach leaves, washed and dried

1½ cups finely chopped flat leaf parsley

1 cup coarsely chopped coriander (cilantro)

1 cup chopped celery leaves

3 garlic cloves, crushed

½ teaspoon sweet paprika

¼ teaspoon chilli powder

3 tablespoons olive oil

½ Preserved Lemon (see page 29), quartered

2 tablespoons lemon juice

6 cherry tomatoes, halved

Harsha (see page 72), Moroccan Dried Black Olives (see page 39) and extra Preserved Lemons (see page 29), to serve

Combine the spinach, parsley, coriander, and celery leaves in a large saucepan. Stir over high heat for about 3 minutes, until wilted. Transfer to colander set over a bowl, press to remove liquid. Place the greens into a glass salad bowl.

Put the reserved spinach liquid into a saucepan, add the garlic, paprika, and chilli powder. Boil, uncovered, over high heat for 3–5 minutes, until reduced slightly. Add the oil, Preserved Lemon and lemon juice.

Spoon the greens onto Harsha (or press into a mould, and unmould onto the Harsha). Place the cherry tomatoes on top and pour the dressing over. Serve with Moroccan Dried Black Olives and Preserved Lemons.

radish, orange and pomegranate salad

Serves 2

	dressing
1 large fennel bulb, sliced with the stalk on	3 tablespoons olive oil
2 oranges, peeled and sliced	2 tablespoons lemon juice
125g radishes, cut into small wedges	2 tablespoons orange juice
½ cup mint leaves	1 tablespoon orange blossom water
pulp of ½ pomegranate	1 teaspoon ground cinnamon
	1 tablespoon icing (confectioners') sugar
	¼ cup (10g/⅓oz) mint leaves

Arrange the fennel slices around the outer edge of a large round serving platter. Working your way to the centre, layer the orange slices overlapping the fennel, place the radish wedges inside the orange slices and the mint leaves in the centre. Sprinkle the pomegranate pulp around the outside.

To make the dressing, blend together the olive oil, juices, orange blossom water, cinnamon, icing (confectioners') sugar and mint leaves. Drizzle over the salad, cover and chill before serving.

carrot sherbet

Serves 4

An interesting salad with a sweet, zesty flavour. Great as a starter, or to cleanse the palate after a spicy meal.

8 firm, crisp carrots	1 tablespoon orange blossom water
juice of 4 large oranges	juice of 1 lemon
1 tablespoon icing (confectioners') sugar	mint leaves, to garnish
½ teaspoon ground cinnamon	

Peel and coarsely grate the outside of the carrots, discarding the hearts. Pour the orange juice over the carrots and mix well.

Sprinkle with icing sugar and cinnamon, add the orange blossom water and lemon juice and mix well. Serve chilled, with mint leaves to garnish.

crispy cumin potato jackets

Serves 4

4 very large potatoes, scrubbed	1 tablespoon cumin seeds
1 sprig thyme	2 eggs
2 teaspoons salt	vegetable oil, for frying

Place the potatoes, thyme and 1 teaspoon of the salt in a saucepan. Cover with water and boil for about 30 minutes, until soft on the inside. Remove from the pan, and cool.

Meanwhile, roast the cumin seeds in a dry frying pan until fragrant, cool then crush in a mortar and pestle.

Leaving the skin on, cut the potatoes in half lengthwise and scoop out most of the flesh (leave about 0.5cm/⅛in of flesh in the jackets). Cut the jackets into bite size pieces.

Mix the cumin and remaining salt together and sprinkle onto the potato jackets. Dip into whisked egg and deep fry in hot oil until crisp. Serve immediately.

Note: You can keep the cooked potato flesh to make mashed potato.

Opposite: Carrot Sherbet

Fried Eggplant (Aubergine) with Spicy Yoghurt and Moroccan Dried Black Olives

Serves 4 (on an mezze platter)

2 long thin eggplants (aubergines),
cut into 1cm (⅜in) rounds
1 tablespoon salt
1 cup (250ml/8fl oz) milk
½ cup (60g/2oz) plain (all purpose) flour
vegetable oil, for frying

marinade

1 Preserved Lemon (see page 29), flesh only
1 tablespoon chopped basil
1 teaspoon ground black pepper
1 tablespoon ground cumin
2 garlic cloves, chopped
½ cup (125ml/4fl oz) olive oil

spicy yoghurt

2 tablespoons olive oil
1 garlic clove, crushed
1 red onion, finely diced
1 green capsicum (bell pepper), seeded and diced
3 firm tomatoes, seeded and diced
2 tablespoons Harissa (see page 26)
2 tablespoons chopped coriander (cilantro)
2 cups (500g/16oz) natural yoghurt

1 cup Moroccan Dried Black Olives (see page 39)
½ Preserved Lemon (see page 29), skin only,
  thinly sliced
½ teaspoon hot paprika

Sprinkle the eggplant (aubergine) slices with salt, stand for 30 minutes to draw out any bitterness; rinse and pat dry. Soak in milk for 2 minutes, then coat lightly with flour to seal. Heat a little oil in a frying pan and cook the slices until golden brown. Set aside to cool.

Combine all the marinade ingredients, coat the cooked eggplant (aubergine) slices in this mixture and marinate for 30 minutes.

Meanwhile, to make the Spicy Yoghurt, heat the olive oil in a saucepan and fry the garlic and onion for 2 minutes. Add the capsicum and tomatoes and cook for 5 minutes, the stir through the Harissa. Take off the heat and set aside to cool. Add the coriander (cilantro) and yoghurt. Mix well and stand for 30 minutes to blend the flavours.

To serve, arrange the eggplant (aubergine) slices in a circle on the outside edge of a large round serving platter. Spoon the Spicy Yoghurt into the centre and arrange the Moroccan Dried Black Olives around the edge of the yoghurt. Garnish with thin strips of Preserved Lemon skin and sprinkle with paprika.

Note: Soaking in milk stops the eggplant from absorbing too much oil and becoming soggy.

desserts,
cakes, pastries
and drinks

sweet couscous seffa

Serves 4

1 cup (250ml/8fl oz) port
1 cup (250ml/8fl oz) water
2 tablespoons caster (superfine) sugar
½ cup (125ml/4fl oz) orange blossom water
1 cinnamon stick
300g (10oz) mixed dried fruit

2 tablespoons icing (confectioners') sugar
500g (1lb) Prepared Couscous (see page 175)
1 tablespoon ground cinnamon
1 cup (90g/3oz) flaked almond, toasted
500g (1lb) natural yoghurt
sprig of mint, to garnish

Combine the port, water, caster (superfine) sugar, orange blossom water and cinnamon stick in a large saucepan and bring to the boil. Cook, stirring occasionally, until reduced by half. Remove from the heat and leave to cool slightly. While still warm, stir through the mixed dried fruit then set aside to cool completely.

Add the icing (confectioners') sugar to the steamed couscous, along with ground cinnamon and half the almonds. Mix gently until combined.

To serve, place the warm couscous on a serving platter. Heap the fruit mixture on the top and drizzle remaining fruit sauce around the outside of the couscous on the plate. Top with the yoghurt and garnish with the remaining almonds and sprig of mint. Serve as a dessert.

Dried Fruit combo with Yoghurt and Almonds

Serves 4

1 cup (250ml/8fl oz) port
2 cups (500ml/16fl oz) water
½ cup (125ml/4fl oz) orange blossom water
½ cup (110g/3¾oz) sugar

250g (8oz) mixed dried fruit
½ cup (125g/4oz) natural yoghurt, toasted
1 tablespoon ground cinnamon
½ cup (45g/1½oz) flaked almonds

Place the port, water, orange blossom water and sugar into a saucepan. Stir to dissolve the sugar, then bring to the boil. Turn down the heat and simmer for 15 minutes, until reduced.

Remove from the heat, add the fruit and stand for about 30 minutes, for the sauce to soak into the fruit. Spoon into bowls, top with a dollop of yoghurt and dust with cinnamon. Sprinkle with almonds, and serve.

Note: The fruit mixture will keep refrigerated for 2 to 3 weeks. You can also serve fruit combo with fresh cream or ice cream, or use it as a crepe filling for breakfast.

strawberry mascarpone pastries

Serves 3

coulis

½ cup (100g/3½oz) brown sugar
1 cup (250ml/8fl oz) water
250g (8oz) strawberries, sliced
¼ cup (60ml/2fl oz) strawberry liqueur
juice of 1 lime
30ml (1fl oz) Cointreau

2 cups (500g) mascarpone cheese
250g (8oz) strawberries, diced

1 sheet frozen puff pastry
1 tablespoon melted butter
1 egg, whisked
6 sliced whole strawberries, mint leaves and icing (confectioners') sugar, to garnish

Preheat the oven to 180°C (350°F/Gas 4). To make the coulis, combine the sugar and water in a saucepan and stir to dissolve. Cook over low heat for 5 minutes then add the sliced strawberries, liqueur, lime juice and Cointreau. Simmer for 10 minutes then set aside to cool. Process in a blender until smooth.

Reserve half of the coulis. Combine the other half with the mascarpone and the diced strawberries. Set aside.

Cut the sheet of pastry into 9 squares. Brush each square with butter, then with egg. Place onto a greased baking tray, and bake for 5 minutes until puffed, golden and crisp. Remove and cool on a cake rack.

Place 1 pastry square into the centre of a serving plate, spoon on some of the mascarpone mixture and top with another pastry square. Spoon on a second layer of mascarpone mixture, top with a third pastry square. Drizzle some of the reserved sauce around the plate, and garnish each one with a sliced strawberry, mint leaves and a dusting of icing sugar.

mhancha

Serves 8–10

The Mhancha gets its name from the word 'hench' which means snake.
It is made with a filling of almond paste rolled in layers of traditional thin pastry
called warka, which is also used to make B'stilla. Filo pastry is an acceptable substitute.

Filling
500g (1lb) blanched almonds
150g (5oz) caster (superfine) sugar
2 tablespoons orange blossom water
150g (5oz) butter, at room temperature
1 egg yolk
1 teaspoon ground cinnamon

16 sheets filo pastry (or warka pastry)
1 egg yolk, lightly whisked
100g (3½oz) butter, melted
200g (6½oz) honey
icing (confectioners') sugar and ground
   cinnamon, to sprinkle

Preheat the oven to 200°C (400°F/Gas 6). To make the filling, put the almonds into a food processor with the caster (superfine) sugar and blend to a paste, add the orange blossom water and blend briefly to combine.

Place the butter into a saucepan with the almond paste and stir over moderate heat for 5 minutes, making sure it doesn't burn. Leave to cool, then add the egg yolk and cinnamon, mix thoroughly.

Shape the almond mixture into 8 long sticks the thickness of your thumb. Brush a pastry sheet with egg yolk and place another sheet on top (the egg will make it stick), place one of the almond logs in the centre and roll the pastry around it to look like a snake. Continue this process until you have 8 'snakes'.

Join the snakes end to end, shaping into a tight spiral, onto a buttered round baking tray. Brush evenly with butter. Bake until golden. Remove from the oven and brush slightly warmed honey all over. Cool before serving and sprinkle with icing (confectioners') sugar and cinnamon.

marinated figs with fresh pomegranate sauce

Serves 4

1¼ cups (310ml/10fl oz) dessert wine	**sauce**
1 cinnamon stick	2 large pomegranates, peeled
1 tablespoon brown sugar	¼ cup (55g/1¼ oz) caster (superfine) sugar
6 figs, halved	¼ cup (60ml/2fl oz) Grenadine
	1 teaspoon lemon juice
	½ cup (125g/4oz) mascarpone

Combine the wine, cinnamon stick and brown sugar in a saucepan and stir over low heat until the sugar dissolves. Place the figs into a glass bowl and pour over the sugar syrup. Cover and stand for 3 hours at room temperature.

To make the sauce, put 1½ pomegranates (keep the remaining ½ pomegranate to garnish) into a food processor with the caster (superfine) sugar and Grenadine, and process until smooth.

Put through a sieve, and stir the lemon juice through the strained sauce.

Drain the figs and char grill the cut side until brown.

Pour pomegranate sauce onto each dessert plate, arrange 3 fig halves on top and serve with a dollop of mascarpone. Garnish with pulp from the reserved pomegranate.

Beghrir

Makes 12

A type of pancake, smooth on one side with little bubbles on the other, Beghrir is very light and will melt in your mouth. In Morocco, earthenware pans are used for cooking Beghrir.

125g (4oz) fine semolina	1 egg, lightly whisked
50g (1¾oz) plain (all purpose) flour, sifted through a very fine sieve	15g (½oz) dried yeast, mixed with 1 tablespoon water
½ teaspoon salt	1 egg, for pan
100ml (3fl oz) milk	butter and honey, to serve
250ml (8fl oz) water	fresh berries or fruit conserve, to serve

Put the semolina and flour into a bowl, add salt. Warm the milk and water over low heat (do not boil), add the egg and yeast. Pour onto the semolina and flour and mix gently for 10 minutes to make a soft batter. Pass through a fine sieve. Cover and leave to prove in a warm place for 2 hours, by which time it should have a frothy appearance on the surface.

Prepare a pancake pan by wiping over with a clean cloth dipped in egg, place over a high heat. Pour in about half a soup ladle of batter and spread lightly over the surface of the pan with the back of the ladle. Cook on one side until thousands of little bubbles appear on the surface. Do not turn, remove gently from the pan with a spatula and place smooth side down on a clean cloth.

Repeat the process above until all mixture is used (do not pile the pancakes on top of each other while they are hot).

To serve, heat a lump of butter in a pan with honey, dip the pancakes in the mixture and place one on top of the other. Serve warm, with fresh berries, or fruit conserve (jelly) sprinkled with icing (confectioners') sugar, if you like.

Baked and stir fried quince

3 cups (675g/1lb 6oz) sugar	50g (1¾oz) butter
1.5L (48fl oz) boiling water	2 tablespoons orange blossom water
1 vanilla bean	2 tablespoons brown sugar
1 cinnamon stick	50g (1¾oz) toasted slivered almonds
4 large quinces, peeled and halved	pistachio ice cream, to serve

Preheat the oven to 150°C (300°F/Gas 2). Combine the sugar and water in a saucepan and stir over low heat until the sugar dissolves. Add the vanilla bean and cinnamon stick.

Place the quinces into a baking dish and pour over the syrup. Cover and bake for 3 hours, until the quinces are soft. Allow the quinces to cool and remove the stones, cut into thick wedges.

Melt the butter in a large frying pan over a medium to high heat. Add the orange blossom water and brown sugar and stir to combine. Add the quince wedges and cook for 2–3 minutes. Stir through the almonds, making sure all the sugar has dissolved and remove from heat. Serve warm or cold, with pistachio ice cream.

Almond Milk

Serves 2

A very refreshing drink for hot summer days.

2 cups (500ml/16fl oz) milk	2 cups (500ml/16fl oz) water
½ cup (110g/3½oz) sugar	¼ cup (60ml/2fl oz) orange blossom water
2 cups (300g/10oz) whole blanched almonds	

Place milk and sugar into a saucepan and stir until the sugar dissolves. Bring to the boil then cool slightly. Put the sweetened milk, almonds and water, 1 cup at a time, into a blender and blend until the almonds are ground. Strain into a jug through a fine-meshed sieve and add the orange blossom water, stir to mix. Serve chilled or over ice cubes.

almond and Raisin Feqqas

Makes about 60

3 eggs	¼ cup (90g/3oz) sultanas (golden raisins)
¼ cup (60ml/2fl oz) vegetable oil	¼ cup (90g/3oz) chopped roasted almonds
½ cup (110g/3½oz) caster (superfine) sugar	2 teaspoons sesame seeds
2 tablespoons orange blossom water	2 teaspoons anise seeds
2 teaspoons baking powder	4 cups (500/1lb) plain (all purpose) flour

Preheat the oven to 135°C (275°F/Gas 1). Combine the eggs, oil, sugar and orange blossom water in a large bowl and whisk until the sugar dissolves. Add the baking powder, sultanas (golden raisins), almonds, sesame and anise seeds and mix well. Add the flour a little at a time and mix to form a firm dough.

Divide the dough into 4 parts and shape each piece into a ball. Place onto a lightly floured surface and using the palm of your hand, shape each ball into a log about 3cm (1¼in) thick. Place onto a greased baking tray and refrigerate for 30 minutes.

Using a sharp knife, cut the logs into 1cm (⅜in) thick slices. Lay out onto greased baking trays and bake for about 45 minutes, until golden and crunchy. Store in an airtight container.

mint Tea

Serves 4

2–3 teaspoons green tea (Chinese gunpowder tea is best)	hot water
fresh mint	sugar, to taste

Measure green tea into a flameproof pot. Pour in a little boiling water, swish around, then immediately strain out (this is just to clean the tea). Wash the mint well and pack tightly into the pot, pour in enough hot water to almost cover the mint. Place pot back onto the stove and bring to the boil.

Remove from the heat and add sugar. Pour out one glass of tea, then pour it back into the pot (this ensures an even mixture of sugar), then repeat this process once more. It is now ready to enjoy!

Serve in glasses as is the tradition, and pour with the pot held high to aerate the tea.

Gazelle's Horns

Makes about 40

Dough

2 cups (250g/8oz) plain (all purpose) flour

½ teaspoon salt

2 tablespoons melted butter

2 tablespoons orange blossom water

1 egg yolk, beaten with a little water

Almond Filling

3 cups (555g/1lb 2oz) ground almonds

2 teaspoons ground cinnamon

1½ cups (180g/6oz) icing (confectioners') sugar

3 tablespoons orange blossom water

6 tablespoons melted butter

1 egg, lightly beaten

½ teaspoon almond essence

½ teaspoon finely grated orange rind

sesame seeds, or icing (confectioners') sugar, to coat

Preheat the oven to 180°C (350°F/Gas 4).

To make the dough, sift the flour and salt into a large mixing bowl and make a well in the centre. Add the melted butter and orange blossom water, mix the dough well, adding the egg mixture a little at a time, until it becomes elastic (about 15 minutes). Set aside.

For the almond filling, combine the almonds, cinnamon and icing (confectioners') sugar in a large bowl. Add the orange blossom water, melted butter, egg, almond essence and rind, and mix to a thick paste. Knead well and break into pieces the size of large apricots. Form each of these pieces into a small sausage shape tapering the ends (you should end up with about 40). Set aside.

To assemble, divide the dough into balls the size of an orange and roll out each on a lightly floured surface. Turn over several times, and roll around the rolling pin, while stretching gently, to form a long ribbon, which is 1mm (¼4in) thick, and a little wider than the filling pieces.

Place the little sausages of almond paste along the dough horizontally, leaving 3–4cm (1¼–1¼in) between each of them, stretch the dough sideways as thinly as possible and fold over to cover the almond sausages. Cut the pastry with a serrated pastry cutter about 2–3mm (⅒ inch) from the filling making crescent (half moon) shapes. Pinch the edges, making sure they are completely sealed. Prick each one with a fork to prevent puffing while cooking.

Repeat this process until all the dough and almond paste is used. Cook for 15–20 minutes until golden. Store in an airtight container.

Serve with Mint Tea (see page 207).

Note: You can either sprinkle with sesame seeds before baking, roll in icing (confectioners') sugar after baking (when cool), or leave plain.

Date and Kahlua Crepes

Serves 6

	sauce
2 eggs	1 cup (180g/6oz) diced fresh dates
300ml (9fl oz) milk	1 cup (250ml/8fl oz) cream
pinch salt	2 tablespoons icing (confectioners') sugar
7 tablespoons plain (all purpose) flour	60ml (2fl oz) Kahlua
1 teaspoon vanilla essence (extract)	60ml (2fl oz) Frangelico
melted butter and oil, to cook	12 whole fresh dates and 12 roasted hazelnuts, to garnish
	cream or ice cream, to serve

Preheat the oven to 150°C (300°F/Gas 2). Whisk the eggs and milk together in a bowl. Add the salt and whisk in the flour a bit at a time, making sure lumps don't develop, add the vanilla essence (extract) and whisk until smooth.

Heat a frying pan until hot, wipe the surface with a mixture of melted butter and oil. Pour on a very thin layer of batter, spreading evenly to cover the base of the pan.

Cook for about 1 minute, until brown. Turn with a spatula and brown the second side for another minute. Repeat until all the batter is used, to make 12 pancakes.

Keep warm in the oven.

To make the sauce, place the dates and cream into a small saucepan. Stir over medium heat until bubbling. Add the icing sugar, continue to stir until the cream starts to turn the colour of the dates. Stir in the Kahlua and Frangelico, take off the heat.

To serve, place a pancake onto a plate with 2 tablespoons of the sauce. Fold and repeat with remaining ingredients, to give 2 pancakes per person. Pour the remaining sauce around each plate, Garnish each with wholes dates stuffed with hazelnuts. Serve with your choice of cream or ice cream.

moroccan chocolate cake

Serves 8

10 egg whites
½ cup (110g/3½oz) caster (superfine) sugar
2 tablespoons self raising (self rising) flour
1 cup chopped (150g/5oz) dark chocolate
1 cup (180g/6oz) chopped fresh dates

1 cup (125g/4oz) chopped roasted almonds
icing (confectioners') sugar, to dust
chocolate sauce, to serve
strawberries, to garnish
ice cream, to serve

Preheat the oven to 200°C (400°F/Gas 6). Grease and line a 22cm (8¾in) round cake tin, 7cm (2¾in) deep.

Whisk the egg whites until stiff while adding the caster sugar and flour a bit at a time (this mixture should resemble that of meringue). Fold in the chocolate, dates and almonds.

Spoon the mixture into the prepared cake tin. Bake the cake for 15 minutes, until the cake rises, then reduce heat to 100°C (200°F/Gas 1) and cook for a further 10 minutes to cook the centre. Cool slightly, then dust with icing (confectioners') sugar. To serve, cut into wedges and drizzle with chocolate sauce. Garnish with strawberries, and serve with ice cream.

poached pears with saffron in rhubarb syrup

Serves 6

6 pears, peeled and cored, with stalks on

1 lemon

2 cups (500ml/16fl oz) white wine

1L (32fl oz) water

2 tablespoons orange blossom water

1¾ cups (400g/14oz) caster (superfine) sugar

2 cinnamon sticks

½ teaspoon saffron threads

1 bunch rhubarb, leaves removed

½ cup (60g/2oz) raisins

Almond and Raisin Feqqas (see page 207), to serve

Place the pears in a bowl and squeeze on lemon juice to prevent them going brown.

Combine the white wine, water, orange blossom water, sugar and cinnamon in a large saucepan; stir to dissolve the sugar. Bring to the boil, reduce the heat and simmer for 15 minutes.

Add the saffron and place the pears into the simmering liquid. Continue to cook for a further 15 minutes, or until the pears are almost cooked. Remove the pears from the saucepan, place into a bowl and pour over half the cooking liquid. Refrigerate overnight to allow the flavours to intensify.

Heat the remaining cooking liquid over low heat, add the rhubarb stalks and cook for 10 minutes. Take out the rhubarb stalks and cinnamon stick, add raisins to the sauce and simmer for 1 minute. Take off the heat and cool.

To serve, place sauce into shallow bowls and stand pears in the middle. Serve with Almond and Raisin Feqqas.

Keneffa

Serves 8

This dessert is served on special occasions. A speciality served at Chez Ali—the famous kazbah in Marakech where movie stars are often seen enjoying a Moroccan Diffa (Feast). The Keneffa served on grand occasions can be over 1 foot high, stacked with pastry, orange blossom custard and cinnamon almonds. Your friends will be amazed at this creation—give it a go for one of your special occasions. Be aware that Keneffa is made to serve straight away—if left too long it becomes soggy.

12 sheets filo pastry (or warka pastry)
200g (7oz) butter

custard

1L (32fl oz) milk
1¼ cups (280g/9½oz) caster (superfine) sugar
200g (6½oz) ground almonds
2 eggs, beaten
3 tablespoons orange blossom water

Almond filling

200g (6½oz) ground almonds
½ cup (60g/2oz) icing (confectioners') sugar
1 teaspoon ground cinnamon
fresh berries, to serve

Cut 8 10cm (4in) rounds from each sheet of pastry. Stick two pastry rounds together by brushing with a little butter. Heat a knob of butter in a frying pan over a low heat. Place the joined pastry rounds into the pan and fry until golden and crisp. Repeat until all the pastry is used.

To make the custard, heat the milk in a saucepan to almost boiling point. Add the sugar and almonds and mix well. Remove from the heat and add the eggs one at a time whisking thoroughly as you go. Add the orange blossom water, put back onto low heat and stir continually while heating through for about 5 minutes, until thickened. Keep warm.

Combine the almond filling ingredients together and set aside.

To assemble the Keneffa, place a pastry layer onto each of 8 serving plates, and sprinkle with almond filling. Cover with another pastry layer then spread on a thin layer of custard. Repeat the layering so that each serve has 6 layers of pastry, with alternating almond and custard layers. Finish with custard and a sprinkle of the almond filling on top.

Serve with fresh berries immediately.

citrus coconut cake
with poppyseeds

Serves 10

	syrup
250g butter, at room temperature	2 oranges
⅔ cup (150g/5oz) caster (superfine) sugar	2 lemons
8 eggs	2 limes
1⅔ (210g/7½oz) cups self raising (rising) flour	1 cup (250ml/8floz) water
¼ cup (100g/3½oz) fine semolina	1 cup (225/7½oz) caster (superfine) sugar
2½ cups (200g/7oz) desiccated coconut	1 cup (250ml/8fl oz) orange juice
1 tablespoon poppyseeds	¼ cup (60ml/2fl oz) Cointreau

Preheat the oven to 180°C (350°F/Gas 4). Grease and line a 25cm (10in) round cake tin.

Cream the butter and sugar until light and fluffy. Add the eggs one at a time, beating well between additions. Sift the flour into a large bowl then add the semolina, coconut and poppy seeds.

Add the flour mixture gradually to the butter mixture, stirring gently to combine, until evenly mixed. Spoon into the prepared tin and bake for 35 minutes. Cool slightly, and turn out onto a wire rack.

To make the syrup, finely grate the rind from one of each of the citrus fruits, and squeeze the juice. Place into a saucepan with the water and sugar. Slowly bring to the boil, stirring to dissolve the sugar. When it boils, reduce the heat and simmer for 10 minutes.

Line a baking tray with non-stick baking paper. Cut the remaining citrus fruits into 5mm (¼in) slices (with the skin on). Dip into the syrup to coat, and place onto the tray. Bake for about 15 minutes, until candied.

Add the orange juice and Cointreau to the syrup, return to the boil. Reduce the heat and simmer for 5 minutes. Arrange the candied fruit slices on top of the cake, and pour the syrup over.

index

First published in Australia in 2004 by
New Holland Publishers (Australia) Pty Ltd
Sydney • Auckland • London • Cape Town

14 Aquatic Drive Frenchs Forest NSW 2086 Australia
218 Lake Road Northcote Auckland New Zealand
86 Edgware Road London W2 2EA United Kingdom
80 McKenzie Street Cape Town 8001 South Africa

10 9 8 7 6 5 4 3 2 1

National Library of Australia Cataloguing-in-Publication Data:

M'Souli, Hassan.
Modern Moroccan.

Includes index.
ISBN 1 74110 115 8.

1. Cookery, Moroccan. I. Title.

641.5964

Managing Editor: Monica Ban
Commissioning Editor: Robynne Millward
Production Controller: Kellie Matterson
Editor: Tracey Rutherford
Designer: Karl Roper
Assistant Writer: Catherine McConachy
Reproduction: Kolorart Graphics
Printer: Everbest Printing, China
Accessories kindly provided by Ambiance Interiors

Out of Africa Restaurant
43–45 East Esplanade
Manly NSW 2095
Ph: 9977 0055   Fax: 9977 2606
Website: www.outofafrica.com.au